JULIUS CÆSAR

JULIUS CÆSAR

William Shakespeare

Edited by
CEDRIC WATTS

WORDSWORTH CLASSICS

For my husband
ANTHONY JOHN RANSON
with love from your wife, the publisher.
Eternally grateful for your unconditional love.

Readers who are interested in other titles from
Wordsworth Editions are invited to visit our website at
www.wordsworth-editions.com

For our latest list and a full mail-order service, contact
Bibliophile Books, 5 Thomas Road, London E14 7BN
TEL: +44 (0)20 7515 9222 FAX: +44 (0)20 7538 4115
E-MAIL: orders@bibliophilebooks.com
WEBSITE: www.bibliophilebooks.com

First published in 1992 by Wordsworth Editions Limited
8B East Street, Ware, Hertfordshire SG12 9HJ

ISBN   978 1 85326 022 3

Wordsworth Editions
is the company founded in 1987 by
MICHAEL TRAYLER

Typeset in Great Britain by Antony Gray
Printed and bound by Clays Ltd, St Ives plc

CONTENTS

GENERAL INTRODUCTION

In the Wordsworth Classics' Shakespeare Series, the inaugural volumes, *Romeo and Juliet*, *The Merchant of Venice* and *Henry V*, have been followed by *The Taming of the Shrew*, *A Midsummer Night's Dream*, *Much Ado about Nothing*, *Julius Cæsar*, *Hamlet*, *Twelfth Night*, *Othello* and *King Lear*. Each play in this Shakespeare Series is accompanied by a standard apparatus, including an introduction, explanatory notes and a glossary. The textual editing takes account of recent scholarship while giving the material a careful reappraisal. The apparatus is, however, concise rather than elaborate. We hope that the resultant volumes prove to be handy, reliable and helpful. Above all, we hope that, from Shakespeare's works, readers will derive pleasure, wisdom, provocation, challenges, and insights: insights into his culture and ours, and into the era of civilisation to which his writings have made – and continue to make – such potently influential contributions. Shakespeare's eloquence will, undoubtedly, re-echo 'in states unborn and accents yet unknown'.

CEDRIC WATTS
Series Editor

INTRODUCTION

> [I]n truth, the period of time covered by history is far too
> short to allow of any perceptible progress in the . . .
> Evolution of the Human Species. The notion that there
> has been any such Progress since Cæsar's time . . . is too
> absurd for discussion. All the savagery . . . exists at the
> present moment.
>
> (George Bernard Shaw.)[1]

I

Shakespeare's *Julius Cæsar* was originally entitled, in the First Folio
of 1623, *The Tragedie of Ivlivs Cæsar.*[2] This might encourage a new
reader to think that the drama would be predominantly about
Cæsar himself; and, indeed, even after being killed (in Act 3), he
continues to influence the action. The play deals not only with his
nature and circumstances, his death at the hands of assassins, and the
varied responses to that death, but also his after-life – both
explicitly, as a ghost, and implicitly, as a character haunting those
who battle to retain the power they have stolen from him. Here we
might see 'the tragedy of a great leader'. Alternatively, one could
argue that Brutus is the main character, for we see far more of him
than we do of Cæsar, and the unfolding action shows how Brutus is
drawn into the conspiracy, participates in the assassination and
offers justification of it; quarrels with Cassius, suffers misfortune in
battle, and eventual dies. (For an accomplished actor, it may well
seem the most attractive rôle in the play.) Here we might see 'the
tragedy of a noble Roman'. A different view has been taken by
Ernest Schanzer, who characterises *Julius Cæsar* as one of three
Shakespearian 'problem plays'. He defines the 'problem play' thus:

A play in which we find a concern with a problem which is central to it, presented in such a manner that we are unsure of our moral bearings, so that uncertain and divided responses to it in the minds of the audience are possible or even probable.

One characteristic of such a play, says Schanzer, is 'dramatic coquetry', which is

the playwright's procedure of manipulating our response to the principal characters, playing fast and loose with our affections for them, engaging and alienating them in turn.[3]

So, on this view, the central problem, which divides us, is whether the assassination of Cæsar was or was not justified; and 'dramatic coquetry' can be observed in the depiction not only of Cæsar himself but also of Brutus, Cassius and Antony. Not surprisingly, then,

Julius Caesar is one of Shakespeare's most controversial plays. Commentators have been quite unable to agree on who is its principal character or whether it has one; on whether it is a tragedy and, if so, of what kind; on whether Shakespeare wants us to consider the assassination as damnable or praiseworthy; while of all the chief characters in the play contradictory interpretations have been given.[4]

Certainly, in Julius Cæsar, Shakespeare, whose next play was quite probably Hamlet, delights in exploring many-sided characters and situations. The treatment of Cæsar himself is intelligently complex. Historically, Julius Cæsar was a combination of genius, war-lord, astute politician and dictator. (In the Orson Welles production of the play in 1937, 'Death of a Dictator' was the topical sub-title.) Undoubtedly courageous and energetic, Cæsar could be both magnanimous and ruthless. Though merciful to some defeated Roman adversaries, he could be appallingly cruel to vanquished foreign foes. He was driven by the desire for wealth and power; and, under his rule, republican Rome, in which corruption had been rife, came to resemble a monarchy ruled by an emperor. (After his death, his family name 'Cæsar', adopted as a title by his successors, became synonymous with 'Emperor', and was eventually employed in that sense, in the forms 'Tsar' and

'Kaiser', by later rulers of Russia and of Germany.) During the subsequent reign of Octavius (Cæsar Octavianus Augustus), republican liberties continued to be subordinated to the power of the ruler; but the arts flourished, so that the term 'The Augustan Age' became synonymous with high achievements in literature, architecture, sculpture and painting.

In the play, Julius Cæsar performs superbly as a public figure who is majestic and almost god-like. He refers to himself in the third person with proud pomposity and lapidary clarity:

> Danger knows full well
> That Cæsar is more dangerous than he.
> We are two lions littered in one day,
> And I the elder and more terrible . . . [5]

Again, he likens himself to the superhuman and transcendent:

> I could be well moved, if I were as you;
> If I could pray to move, prayers would move me;
> But I am constant as the Northern Star,
> Of whose true fixed and resting quality
> There is no fellow in the firmament.

From one point of view, such claims are arrogant and tempt fate; from another point of view, Cæsar is highly conscious of his rôle as an extraordinary leader – indeed, as a historical force – and his rhetoric is aptly expressive. If there is a degree of arrogance, there are also telling instances of various positive qualities. One is a form of modesty, even fatal modesty: 'What touches us ourself shall be last served', he remarks, putting aside a crucial warning (but using the royal plural). Another is his hospitable warmth: 'Good friends, go in and taste some wine with me', he cordially invites the conspirators. And another is his knowledgeable concern for his fellow-men, as when, using the ominous adjective 'lean', he tells Caius Ligarius: 'Cæsar was ne'er so much your enemy / As that same ague which hath made you lean.' His judgements of people are sometimes too trusting, but sometimes incisively astute: 'Yond Cassius hath a lean and hungry look; / He thinks too much: such men are dangerous.' He shows courage in facing enemies, for, even when being stabbed to death, he can utter a telling reproach: '*Et tu, Brute?*': 'Even you, Brutus?'.

Cæsar's significance seems to be confirmed by the supernatural. On the eve of the assassination, we find that, amid thunder and lightning, a bizarre series of supernatural phenomena assails Rome: a lioness gives birth in the streets, graves yawn and yield up their dead, warriors fight on clouds, blood drizzles on the Capitol, men walk about in flames, and ghosts shriek and squeal. Classical Rome has been invaded by Gothic nightmares. As Calphurnia points out, dying beggars don't get this kind of show; it looks like a resounding metaphysical fanfare for Cæsar's imminent downfall. The greater the supernatural fuss, the more important the victim.[6] In the first scene of *Hamlet*, just before the ghost of Hamlet's father returns, Horatio recalls the apparitions which appeared in Rome before Cæsar's death: these, he says, were produced by 'heaven and earth together' as 'harbingers preceding still the fates'.

If Cæsar aspires to the god-like, he is inevitably human, and therefore mortal and fallible. After declaring proudly to Antony,

> I rather tell thee what is to be feared,
> Than what I fear; for always I am Cæsar[,]

he adds:

> Come on my right hand, for this ear is deaf . . .

Human weakness is again apparent when, after Calphurnia dissuades him from going to the Capitol, he is persuaded to go by Decius, who says that the Senate intends to bestow a crown on him. (There is no reason to doubt Caska's claim[7] that Cæsar had previously been annoyed when most of the spectators at the Lupercalia applauded his rejection of a crown.) Of course, the contrast between 'Cæsar the Great' and 'Cæsar the fallible mortal' has been exploited by Cassius when seeking to win Brutus to the conspiracy. In that 'temptation scene', Cassius says:

> this man
> Is now become a god, and Cassius is
> A wretched creature, and must bend his body
> If Cæsar carelessly but nod on him.
> He had a fever when he was in Spain,
> And when the fit was on him, I did mark
> How he did shake: 'tis true, this god did shake . . .

He delights in claiming that Cæsar, having challenged Cassius to a swimming contest, nearly drowned and called for help. Another conspirator, Caska, notes with relish how Cæsar, in public, was humiliated by collapsing in an epileptic fit. The effect on us, the audience, however, may not be what the conspirators would wish. They would like people to respond: 'How dare such a fallible person behave like a god!'. But our response may well be, 'Of course Cæsar is only human, but these reminders of his fallibility and his illness help to make him more sympathetic: indeed, his achievements may seem all the greater, since he has striven to overcome his limitations. Furthermore, the gloating pleasure which the conspirators take in the man's misfortunes makes them appear callous and malicious.' Later, with poetic justice, Cassius is revealed to be both physically and intellectually myopic: 'My sight was ever thick', he confesses.

A telling (though unintentional) defence of Cæsar actually comes from Cassius, when he says:

> Cæsar doth bear me hard; but he loves Brutus.
> If I were Brutus now, and he were Cassius,
> He should not humour me.

In other words, 'I have reason to be resentful against Cæsar, but Brutus does not. If I were in Brutus' position, I would not be won over by Cassius.'[8] As for Brutus: when he is considering Cassius' arguments, he reflects:

> Th'abuse of greatness is when it disjoins
> Remorse from power; and, to speak truth of Cæsar,
> I have not known when his affections swayed
> More than his reason.

There he considers that, although great men become bad when they become ruthless, in Julius Cæsar, on the contrary, emotion is always governed by reason: in other words, Cæsar governs well. It's a remarkable confession. (In fact, the historic Cæsar, who became 'Perpetual Dictator' a month before his death, was guilty of a blatant lust for power, of barbaric cruelty to defeated enemies, and of the erosion of republican liberties; but Brutus, who 'love[s] him well', does not seem to have noticed any of these.[9]) Why, then, does Brutus join the conspirators? He does so because he is persuaded by the argument that Cæsar may become tyrannical if allowed to live. Brutus has the reputation of being an honourable man, but his logic is poor. The argument that a person 'may become' bad is an utterly inadequate justification for murder.[10] On the basis of such logic, anyone could be murdered. Brutus' confusion is evident when he says:

> We all stand up against the spirit of Cæsar,
> And in the spirit of Cæsar there is no blood:
> O, that we then could come by Cæsar's spirit,
> And not dismember Cæsar! But alas,
> Cæsar must bleed for it.

Here Brutus both separates and unites the spirit and body of Cæsar. An astute critic, George Watson, has remarked:

> Can one destroy the spirit of Cæsar by spilling his blood? . . .
> Throughout the play, Shakespeare stresses the illogicality of
> Brutus' position by showing that there is no necessary correlation
> between the spirit and the frail body.

The very first scene shows that physical death has not lessened the influence of Pompey's spirit on Flavius and Murellus.

> The scene suggests the pervasiveness of 'Cæsarism' – and
> possibly its inevitability – in the Roman state, not just by
> showing us the monarchical sentiments of the Plebeians, but by
> emphasising that the Tribunes themselves, opponents of Cæsar
> as they may be, are thoroughly Cæsarist in their attitudes to
> Pompey.[11]

The assassination is treacherous and cowardly: numerous men, some of whom have been favoured by Cæsar, now stab the unarmed leader. Brutus ventures the absurd argument that the conspirators are Cæsar's friends, for they 'have abridged / His time of fearing death'. Then he urges the assassins to smear themselves in Cæsar's blood and walk about shouting 'Peace, freedom and liberty!'. The bloodstained corpse of Cæsar comments mutely but tellingly on the slogans. Then Cassius cries:

> How many ages hence
> Shall this our lofty scene be acted over,
> In states unborn and accents yet unknown?

It's a splendidly self-validating comment. In the imaginary world of ancient Rome, he asks whether the assassination will be commemorated in theatres down the ages. Well, of course, it *has* been, notably in this play by Shakespeare called *Julius Cæsar*. The 'states unborn' include the U.S.A., Canada, Australia and the Russian Federation; the accents 'yet unknown' to the Romans would include modern American, Japanese and Mandarin. An unintended irony is, of course, that the scene of political assassination will be repeated not only on stage but also in historical actuality. Cassius unwittingly reminds us of the many murders which scar political history: famous victims include Jean Paul Marat, Abraham Lincoln, Tsar Alexander II, President Garfield, President Carnot, King Umberto, President McKinley, King Alexander, Tsar Nicholas II and his family, Leon Trotsky, Mahatma Gandhi, John F. Kennedy, Robert Kennedy, Martin Luther King, Anwar Sadat and Indira Gandhi. Enthusiastically entering the self-referential game, Brutus caps Cassius' question with one of his own:

> How many times shall Cæsar bleed in sport,
> That now on Pompey's basis lies along,
> No worthier than the dust?

Yes, Cæsar will bleed 'in sport', in entertainments (such as this one); but he will be declared a god by the Roman authorities, and he will be granted a historic immortality which will mock the conspirators' arrogance. After Brutus' speech to exculpate the assassins, a plebeian's shout unwittingly undercuts all he has said: 'Let him be Cæsar!'.

Furthermore, Mark Antony will soon persuade the crowd that Cæsar was far worthier than any of his assassins; and what the conspirators had imagined to be a new era of 'peace and freedom' becomes a time of civil war in which Brutus and Cassius will be destroyed by the forces of Octavius and Antony. Shakespeare was fond of dramatising a large-scale political irony in which the killing of a legitimate ruler unleashes havoc and brings woe upon the killer or killers. (The political implications are not necessarily conservative: the plays can be diversely interpreted; and they are works of entertainment, not pieces of propaganda.) In the sequence of history plays which emerged between 1595 and 1599, consisting of

Richard II, *Henry IV Part 1* and *Part 2*, and *Henry V*, Shakespeare had shown how the deposition and murder of an anointed king, Richard II, results in civil war; the usurper, Henry IV, becomes a worried, weary, guilty monarch; and not until the era of Henry V does it seem that God relents and forgives. Later, in *Hamlet* (*c.* 1600), Claudius murders Hamlet's father and gains the throne, but other deaths ensue, and within months he is slain. Later still, in *Macbeth* (*c.* 1604), Macbeth finds that his killing of Duncan brings him only more trouble, bloodshed, and, eventually, death at the hands of Duncan's avengers. Accordingly, in *Julius Cæsar*, the conspirators make things worse, not better, as Cinna, the poet, soon discovers. George Watson has commented that 'the spirit of Cæsar is even more potent once the man himself is dead'; indeed, 'The whole of the latter part of the play – Acts IV and V – might well be called "Cæsar's Revenge".'[12] Antony had prophesied that Cæsar's spirit would come 'ranging for revenge'; Cæsar's ghost appears to Brutus; and both Brutus and Cassius, dying, eventually feel that they have been overcome by Cæsar rather than by Antony and Octavius. Cassius says:

> Cæsar, thou art revenged,
> Even with the sword that killed thee.

Brutus says:

> Cæsar, now be still;
> I killed not thee with half so good a will.

If disgust at the assassination of Cæsar makes us sympathetic to the courageous Antony and his brilliant rhetoric, Shakespeare provides a chilling rebuff in Act 4, scene 1, where we find that Antony, Octavius and Lepidus are ruthless in selecting individuals to be murdered: even Lepidus' brother and Antony's nephew are not spared. Furthermore, Antony intends to manipulate Cæsar's publicly-spirited will, which had figured so prominently in his oratory to the crowd, to finance the campaign. In *Antony and Cleopatra*, the victorious triumvirate will fall to dissension, Lepidus will be demoted, and eventually Antony will die, defeated by the ruthless and calculating Octavius. Even before the end of *Julius Cæsar*, however, there are portents of that dissension. In 4.1.18-27, Antony persuades Octavius to conspire with him against Lepidus, and at 5.1.16–20, Octavius insists bluntly on over-ruling Antony's tactical judgement. 'Why do you cross me in this exigent?', asks Antony, and Octavius replies in haughty terms which echo Julius Cæsar: 'I do not cross you; but I *will* do so.'

Audiences readily sympathise with underdogs, and Brutus and Cassius become more sympathetic as they face defeat. Their quarrel, while exposing the moral laxity of Cassius, has exposed not only the contrasts between the two characters but also their complementarity, and their reconciliation shows that they are capable at times of deep friendship. In their suicidal deaths, they perhaps atone for their murder of Cæsar. Antony's rhetoric is not always to be trusted, but his tribute to the dead Brutus has some validity:

> All the conspirators, save only he,
> Did that they did in envy of great Cæsar;
> He, only, in a general honest thought,
> And common good to all, made one of them.

Even when Brutus and Cassius are dead, the action is not complete. The sequence of political matters which began at the opening of *Julius Cæsar* will not end until, at the close of *Antony and Cleopatra*, Octavius pronounces his judgement:

> She shall be buried by her Antony.
> No grave upon the earth shall clip in it
> A pair so famous.

So, when we look back over *Julius Cæsar*, we may feel that it is inappropriate to ask 'Who is the tragic hero?', for Cæsar, Brutus, Cassius, Caska, Calphurnia, Portia and numerous other characters (including, touchingly, Cinna the poet) have all contributed to an unfolding drama which is at once historic, tragic, political, moral and psychological. The interplay of the general and the particular, of the public actions and the private tensions, of historic display and intimate moments, is finely orchestrated. This is a mature, sophisticated, austere and elegant work; though the elegance is achieved at some dramatic cost, because ancient Rome has no Falstaff, Tearsheet, Pistol or Boar's Head Tavern. For all its complexity, the play is not as uncertain and baffling in its nature as Ernest Schanzer's argument might suggest. Whether seen from a moral or a practical viewpoint, the assassins of Cæsar are wrong.[13] Schanzer's term 'dramatic coquetry' suggests a presentation of characters which is teasingly and frustratingly unresolved; but the play enables us to form, eventually, clear judgements of all the major figures; and all are flawed.

A modern historian's verdict on the real Cæsar and his opponents is this:

> To be ruled by Caesar meant submission to a thoroughgoing autocrat, who was quite capable of visiting the most ruthless punishment on anyone who got out of line – a line drawn by himself. To be ruled, on the other hand, by the noblemen of the late Republic meant subjection to the wills of a corrupt, self-seeking, arrogant caucus of noblemen, whose slogan 'liberty' referred exclusively to their own unrestricted freedom of action and speech, and no one else's. Neither of these two different kinds of domination could be described as in the least desirable for its victims, and to build up either Caesar or his political enemies as saintly heroes, or, after their downfall, as saintly martyrs, is entirely misleading. On balance, perhaps most of us would have preferred living under Caesar, whose administrative measures at least showed some concern for the welfare of the ordinary Roman.[14]

'Not much of a choice, though', democrats may reflect.

2

Shakespeare's main source for *Julius Cæsar* was Sir Thomas North's translation of Plutarch's *The Lives of the Noble Grecians and Romanes* (1579), a mixture of fact and legend tinged with fiction. From that large body of material, Shakespeare selected passages connected with the downfall of Cæsar. He compressed the time-scale of events from three years to (apparently) a few weeks, intensified the action, and magnified the sense of social life (notably by giving greater prominence to the plebeians). Shakespeare increased the inwardness of certain characters, notably Brutus and Cassius. Brutus' soliloquy at the opening of Act 2 does not have a counterpart in Plutarch's pages, and, by expanding Plutarch's more sparse account of the 'temptation', he made Brutus more troubled and reflective. The finely-modulated scene of the quarrel between Cassius and Brutus (Act 4, scene 2) brought new realism to the depiction of a relationship under stress: the tones run a fluently-modulated gamut between rage and love.

Julius Cæsar is one of the most intelligent, eloquent and memorable political plays ever written. Politically, it remains strikingly cogent. Although it 'mystifies' by supernatural devices the status of Cæsar, to a large extent its view of history is sceptical and unillusioned, and therefore persuasive. One theme of the play is that numerous valuable human qualities – love, affection, kindness, loyalty – are subverted and wasted in the course of political machinations. The critic L. C. Knights has claimed that *Julius Cæsar* and *Coriolanus* together suggest two truths:

> The first is that human actuality is more important than any political abstraction, though more difficult to bear. The second is that politics is vitiated and corrupted to the extent to which, as politicians, we lose our sense of the *person* on the other side of the dividing line of class or party or nation.[15]

To this day, human beings are, all too often, sacrificed pointlessly on the altar of one political ideology or another. Again and again, men of slogans and ambition seduce and delude their more decent auditors; the many are swayed by the hypocritical rhetoric of the few. Repeatedly, violence generates yet more violence. Again and again, a cruel means corrupts an apparently good end. Certainly, some wars were worth fighting, notably the war of 1939–45 to defend democracy against the fascist alliance of Nazi Germany, Mussolini's Italy and Hirohito's Japan. But *Julius Cæsar* may remind us that in Britain in the 17th century, the Civil War, in which Charles I was executed, resulted not in liberty from oppression but in the autocratic 'Protectorate' of Oliver Cromwell. (Within a few years, the monarchy was restored; so thousands of lives had, it appeared, been pointlessly lost.) The play may remind us, too, that the French Revolution, with its watchwords of '*Liberté, Égalité, Fraternité*', resulted in the carnage of the guillotine, the invasion of republican Switzerland by the revolutionary army, and eventually in the emergence of Napoléon as autocratic emperor. It may remind us that the communistic ideals of the Russian revolutionaries were mocked by the subsequent tyranny of Joseph Stalin, and that the Chinese revolutionaries paved the way for the ruthlessly erratic dictatorship of Chairman Mao, whose 'People's Army' invaded and conquered Tibet in 1950–51 and attacked India in 1962. For us, today, therefore, there is a peculiarly grim irony in the sanguine hopes of Brutus and Cassius that their deeds will be re-enacted 'in states unborn and accents yet unknown'. Shakespeare's bloodstained conspirators have indeed proven to be truer prophets, alas, than they could ever have foreseen. If more people read *Julius Cæsar*, perhaps fewer people will die in vain.

The play was termed a 'Tragedie' in the First Folio. Historically, 'Tragedy' is the name given to an evolving family of works. The family's identity is constituted by a number of features which make a pattern of 'family resemblances'. Some works have all of those features, and we confidently call them tragedies. Other works have fewer of them, and we may hesitate before specifying their genre. Families interbreed in nature and in culture, so that a single work may inhabit several genres; or it may resemble a rebellious offspring, linked to its parents by antipathy, but shaped by their characteristics. A literary tragedy is a work which embodies well problems associated with human suffering. One problem may be that of theodicy: how can belief in divine justice be reconciled with evidence of worldly injustice? Another may be existential: how can the desire for significance in life be reconciled with evidence of the insignificance or absurdity of human existence? Often the action is radically ironic: we see energies turned against themselves, downfall causally related to aspiration, and limitations emphasised by capacities and potentialities. Consolatory features often include the cumulative patterning of events and the engaging articulacy of their presentation, though some works of the genre may deny us such consolations. A tragedy may deal with the problems of a group of people; and it may portray a historical process rather than a suffering individual. So, if one wished to confer on *Julius Cæsar* a prestigious generic title, it sufficiently earns the title 'tragedy'. It also belongs, however, to the genres of revenge drama, the history play and the political drama, to the sub-genre of the Roman Play, and, in some stagings (which have employed hundreds and even thousands of performers), to the popular genre of the epic spectacular; and it is tinged by black comedy or tragic farce.[16]

While not being as deeply problematic as Ernest Schanzer suggested, *Julius Cæsar* is a 'problem play' in the mild sense that the mixture of qualities in Cæsar, Brutus, Cassius and Antony repeatedly complicates our moral and political judgements. Bertolt Brecht, reputedly a Marxist dramatist, used to argue that traditional tragedy was conservative because it made people think 'Human nature doesn't change; there's nothing to be done, alas'. Instead, following the example of George Bernard Shaw,[17] Brecht advocated a theatre which would induce not emotional reverie but critical reflection on the world and a desire to change it. Repeatedly, when seeking precedent for such a theatre, Brecht invoked the Elizabethan dramatists and, in particular, Shakespeare.[18] *Julius Cæsar*, which both mystifies and demystifies political leadership, is a good illustration of what he had in mind. One of the ironies of *Julius Cæsar* is that its own seductively eloquent rhetoric warns us to be critical of seductively eloquent rhetoric in the political world. The warning remains timely.

NOTES ON THE INTRODUCTION

1 George Bernard Shaw: 'Notes' to *Three Plays for Puritans* (London: Constable, 1911), p. 203. I preserve the inconsistent capitalisation ('progress . . . Progress').

2 I preserve the First Folio's spelling, in which 'I' and 'v' sometimes serve as 'J' and 'u'.

3 Ernest Schanzer: *The Problem Plays of Shakespeare: A Study of 'Julius Caesar', 'Measure for Measure', 'Antony and Cleopatra'* (Routledge & Kegan Paul, 1963; rpt. 1965), pp. 6 and 70.

4 Schanzer, p. 10. Though I spell 'Cæsar' with a diphthong, I preserve the alternative spelling ('Caesar') where another writer has used it.

5 Cæsar is not alone in referring to himself in the third person (which he does nineteen times): Brutus and Cassius (numerous times), Mark Antony (four), Caska and Portia (once each) do so: they thus emphasise their awareness of their personal dignity and public rôles.

6 Shakespeare was magnifying what he found in Plutarch, who mentions spirits running about, men 'going up and down in fire', and other supernatural phenomena.

7 'Caska' (rather than the customary 'Casca') is the First Folio's spelling.

8 An alternative reading of the lines would make the 'He' refer to Cæsar, but this reading seems far less apt.

9 Around 1818, Samuel Taylor Coleridge remarked indignantly: 'How too could Brutus say, he finds no personal cause[;] i.e. none in Caesar's past conduct . . . ? Had he not passed the Rubicon? Entered Rome as a conqueror? Placed his Gauls in the Senate?' See *Marginalia IV*, ed. H. J. Jackson and George Whalley (Princeton, N. J.: Princeton University Press, 1998), p. 807.

10 It may remind us of the claim made by some western politicians in 2003: that Saddam Hussein might use weapons of mass destruction in the future, and therefore his country, Iraq, should be invaded in the present..

11 George Watson: 'The Spirit of Cæsar', in *Longman Critical Essays: 'Julius Cæsar': William Shakespeare*, ed. Linda Cookson and Bryan Loughrey (Harlow: Longman, 1992), p. 92 (both quotations).

12 Watson, pp. 93 and 94.

13 As autocrats are often unpopular, numerous stage-productions (particularly eighteenth-century productions) have adjusted the text to make Brutus appear a patriotic tragic hero.

14 Michael Grant: *Great Lives: Caesar* (London: Weidenfeld & Nicolson and Book Club Associates, 1974), pp. 12–13.

15 L. C. Knights: 'Shakespeare and Political Wisdom: A Note on the Personalism of *Julius Caesar*', in *Twentieth Century Interpretations of 'Julius Caesar'*, ed. Leonard F. Dean (Englewood Cliffs, N. J.: Prentice-Hall, 1968), p. 54.

16 Herbert Beerbohm Tree employed over 250 performers in a production in 1898, while in 1916 a production at the Beechwood Amphitheater near Los Angeles used about 5000. See *Julius Caesar*, ed. Marvin Spevack (Cambridge: Cambridge University Press, 1988), p. 34, and John Ripley's *'Julius Caesar' on Stage in England and America 1599–1973* (Cambridge: Cambridge University Press, 1980), p. 221. As for 'black comedy' and 'tragic farce': consider the conduct of the fickle crowd, both comic and violent, or the fact that Cassius' death results from a fatally pessimistic interpretation of a joyful situation.

17 Shaw said: '[M]y plays are built to induce, not voluptuous reverie but intellectual interest, not romantic rhapsody but humane concern', and he remarked that they were heralded by some of Shakespeare's plays in which 'we find him ready and willing to start at the twentieth century if the seventeenth would only let him'. See his *Plays Unpleasant: 'Widowers' Houses', 'The Philanderer', 'Mrs Warren's Profession'* [1898], as reprinted with later comments (Harmondsworth: Penguin, 1965), pp. 196 and 22.

18 See, for example: Bertolt Brecht: *The Messingkauf Dialogues*, translated by John Willett (London: Methuen, 1965), especially pp. 57–64. (Brecht was awarded the 'Stalin Peace Prize' two years after the Berlin Uprising of 1953.)

FURTHER READING
(in chronological order)

Harley Granville-Barker: *Prefaces to Shakespeare: First Series* [1927]. London: Sidgwick & Jackson, 1945.

G. Wilson Knight: *The Imperial Theme*. London: Oxford University Press, 1931; rpt., London: Methuen, 1985.

D. A. Traversi: *Shakespeare: The Roman Plays*. London: Hollis & Carter, 1963.

Ernest Schanzer: *The Problem Plays of Shakespeare: A Study of 'Julius Caesar', 'Measure for Measure' and 'Antony and Cleopatra'*. London: Routledge & Kegan Paul, 1963.

Narrative and Dramatic Sources of Shakespeare: Vol. V: The Roman Plays, ed. Geoffrey Bullough. London: Routledge & Kegan Paul; New York: Columbia University Press; 1964.

Discussions of Shakespeare's Roman Plays, ed. Maurice Charney. Boston: Heath, 1965.

Twentieth Century Interpretations of 'Julius Caesar': A Collection of Critical Essays, ed. Leonard F. Dean. Englewood Cliffs, N. J.: Prentice-Hall, 1968.

Shakespeare: 'Julius Caesar': A Casebook, ed. Peter Ure. London: Macmillan, 1969.

J. L. Simmons: *Shakespeare's Pagan World: The Roman Tragedies*. Hassocks, Brighton: Harvester Press, 1974.

David Daiches: *Shakespeare: Julius Caesar*. London: Arnold, 1976.

Samuel Schoenbaum: *William Shakespeare: A Compact Documentary Life*. London and New York: Oxford University Press, 1977; rpt., 1987.

John Ripley: *'Julius Caesar' on Stage in England and America 1599-1973*. Cambridge: Cambridge University Press, 1980.

Robin H. Wells: *Shakespeare, Politics and the State*. Basingstoke: Macmillan, 1986.

The Cambridge Companion to Shakespeare Studies, ed. Stanley Wells. Cambridge: Cambridge University Press, 1986.

Alexander Leggatt: *Shakespeare's Political Drama: The History Plays and the Roman Plays*. London: Methuen, 1989.

Longman Critical Essays: 'Julius Caesar': William Shakespeare, ed. Linda Cookson and Bryan Loughrey. Harlow: Longman, 1992.

Vivian Thomas: *Julius Caesar*. Hemel Hempstead: Harvester Wheatsheaf, 1992.

Richard Wilson: *Will Power: Essays on Shakespearean Authority*. Brighton: Harvester Wheatsheaf, 1993.

Geoffrey Miles: *Shakespeare and the Constant Romans*. Oxford: Oxford University Press, 1996.

Shakespeare: The Roman Plays, ed. Graham Holderness, Bryan Loughrey and Andrew Murphy. Harlow: Longman, 1996.

Coppélia Kahn: *Roman Shakespeare: Warriors, Wounds and Women*. London: Routledge, 1997.

Mary Hamer: *William Shakespeare: Julius Caesar*. Plymouth: Northcote House, 1998.

Kenneth S. Rothwell: *A History of Shakespeare on Screen: A Century of Film and Television*. Cambridge: Cambridge University Press, 1999.

John Sutherland and Cedric Watts: *Henry V, War Criminal? and Other Shakespeare Puzzles*. Oxford: Oxford University Press, 2000.

New Casebooks: Julius Caesar: William Shakespeare, ed. Richard Wilson. Basingstoke: Palgrave, 2002.

Shakespeare: An Oxford Guide, ed. Stanley Wells and Lena Cowen Orlin. Oxford: Oxford University Press, 2003.

NOTE ON SHAKESPEARE

William Shakespeare was the son of a glover at Stratford-upon-Avon, and tradition gives his date of birth as 23 April, 1564; certainly, three days later, he was christened at the parish church. It is likely that he attended the local Grammar School but had no university education. Of his early career there is no record, though John Aubrey reports a claim that he was a rural schoolmaster. In 1582 Shakespeare married Anne Hathaway, with whom he had two daughters, Susanna and Judith, and a son, Hamnet, who died in 1596. How he became involved with the stage in London is uncertain, but by 1592 he was sufficiently established as a playwright to be criticised in print as a challengingly versatile 'upstart Crow'. He was a leading member of the Lord Chamberlain's company, which became the King's Men on the accession of James I in 1603. Being not only a playwright and actor but also a 'sharer' (one of the owners of the company, entitled to a share of the profits), Shakespeare prospered greatly, as is proven by the numerous records of his financial transactions. Towards the end of his life, he loosened his ties with London and retired to New Place, the large house in Stratford-upon-Avon which he had bought in 1597. He died on 23 April, 1616, and is buried in the place of his baptism, Holy Trinity Church. The earliest collected edition of his plays, the First Folio, was published in 1623, and its prefatory verse-tributes include Ben Jonson's famous declaration, 'He was not of an age, but for all time'.

ACKNOWLEDGEMENTS AND TEXTUAL MATTERS

I have consulted – and am indebted to – numerous editions of *Julius Cæsar*, notably those by: John Dover Wilson ('The New Shakespeare': London: Cambridge University Press, 1949; revised and abridged as 'The Cambridge Pocket Shakespeare', 1957, reprinted 1967); Peter Alexander (London and Glasgow: Collins, 1951; rpt. 1966); T. S. Dorsch ('The Arden Shakespeare': London: Methuen, 1955; rpt. 1965); Arthur Humphreys ('The Oxford Shakespeare': Oxford: Oxford University Press, 1984); Stanley Wells and Gary Taylor (*The Complete Works*: Oxford: Oxford University Press, 1986); Marvin Spevack ('The New Cambridge Shakespeare': Cambridge: Cambridge University Press, 1988); John F. Andrews ('The Everyman Shakespeare': London: Dent, 1993); Stephen Greenblatt *et al.* (*The Norton Shakespeare*: New York and London: Norton, 1997); and David Danniell ('The Arden Shakespeare', 3rd Series: Walton-on-Thames: Nelson, 1998). The Glossary of this volume adapts and revises Dover Wilson's. In the annotations, the citations of Plutarch are from his *The Lives of the Noble Grecians and Romanes*, translated by Sir Thomas North (London, 1579), but I have modernised the spelling and punctuation.

I turn now to some textual details: they may seem dry at first, but you will soon see their importance. The terms 'quarto' and 'folio' crop up. A 'quarto' is a book with relatively small pages, while a 'folio' is a book with relatively large pages. A quarto volume is made of sheets of paper, each of which has been folded twice to form four leaves (and thus eight pages), whereas each of a folio's sheets has been folded once to form two leaves (and thus four pages). Whereas many other Shakespearian plays exist in early quartos as well as in folio form, the earliest surviving text of *Julius Cæsar* is that found in the First Folio of 1623, which was published seven years after the playwright's death. That First Folio (often designated 'F1') was the original 'collected edition' of Shakespeare's plays, assembled by two of the fellow-actors in his company, John Heminge (or Heminges) and Henry Condell. The fact that there is no quarto text to compare with the F1 text might appear to make the editor's task easier, for there is not the problem of deciding between quite different readings. (The variations between different copies of F1 are few and small.) On the other hand, the editor's task is also harder, in the sense that there are no authoritative alternatives to consider if the copy-text seems faulty or obscure; and, in any case, posterity may thus lack some Shakespearian material that a quarto would have preserved. A Shakespearian play did not spring into existence fully-formed; it evolved. You can see good evidence of this in Act 4, scene 2, of *Julius Cæsar*.

In that scene, the death of Brutus' wife, Portia, is announced twice. The first occasion occurs when, after Cassius says that Brutus does not live up to his stoical philosophy, Brutus reveals to Cassius that Portia has died. Cassius, shocked, exclaims: 'How scaped I killing, when I crossed you so?' Brutus then explains that she had committed suicide, partly because she missed Brutus and partly because she grieved that Antony and Octavius, his foes, were gaining strength. She had 'swallowed fire' to die. 'O ye immortal gods!', responds Cassius; but Brutus, stoically enough, says: 'Speak no more of her. Give me a bowl of wine.' Five lines later, Titinius and Messala enter; and, in the course of the conversation, Brutus expresses the suspicion that Messala is concealing what he knows of Portia. The second announcement then follows, as Messala says: 'For certain she is dead, and by strange manner.' Brutus briskly responds:

> Why, farewell, Portia. – We must die, Messala:
> With meditating that she must die once,
> I have the patience to endure it now.

'Even so great men great losses should endure', remarks Messala, approving the stoical response.

One way of explaining this repetition is to say that Brutus' hypocrisy is being revealed. Although he knows that Portia is dead, he pretends to Messala that he is hearing the news for the first time, so that he can make a practised stoical reply, thus earning Messala's approval. In that case, however, Cassius would hardly have said

> I have as much of this in art as you,
> But yet my nature could not bear it so.

This means: 'In theory I'm a Stoic, too, but in practice I could not carry the matter off as you do.' It seems unlikely that he would thus endorse Brutus' deception of Messala. A more likely response from Cassius would be a sharply critical protest at such duplicity. Another way of explaining the repetition, and one favoured by numerous editors, is to claim that after writing one version, Shakespeare changed his mind and wrote an alternative version, and, though one was supposed to be cancelled, both versions have erroneously been preserved in print. There is precedent for such duplication. In *Love's Labour's Lost*, we find both revised and unrevised versions of a passage in Act 4, scene 3, and of another passage in Act 5, scene 2. Of course, those who think that *Julius Cæsar*, Act 4, scene 2, present Shakespeare's first and second thoughts have the problem of deciding which passage is the 'cancelled' one. Curiously, both look like later insertions into the scene. If lines 193–208 are ignored, the text runs fluently: Lucius is asked to supply a bowl of wine, and Brutus proceeds to pledge his renewed friendship to Cassius as a toast. (Lucius would not need to go out for wine, which would naturally have been found in Brutus' tent.) If, alternatively, lines 231–45 are ignored, the text again runs fluently. After Messala has noted that Cicero is dead, Brutus aptly comments, 'Well, to our work alive.' You may think that passage 231–45 depicts Brutus as too severe, and that passage 193–208 represents Shakespeare's improvement, a more elaborate treatment which is true to the relatively mild character of Brutus (who concedes the greatness of his sorrow) and which aptly completes the reconciliation of Brutus with Cassius. The integration of the fuller material is completed with Cassius' 'Portia, art thou gone?' at 216: he is still musing on the shocking news.

So, if you are staging the play, you have at least four options here. You could keep both the passages, giving the audience an insight into an unexpected deviousness on the part of Brutus. The second option would be to cut lines 231–45, thus accentuating the fairly gentle Brutus and his reconciliation with the sympathetic Cassius. The third option would be to cut lines 193–208, to show Brutus as toughly, almost ruthlessly, stoical. The fourth would be to delete the two passages and save time. I've kept them to be true to F1 and to give you the choice. Their preservation here does not necessarily imply that I would stage them both.

Compared with the other plays in the First Folio, the text of *Julius Cæsar* is of very high quality. There are relatively few misprints, the punctuation is less often misleading, and the misattribution of speeches seldom occurs. Although textual corruption can be postulated (e.g. at 1.3.129, 2.1.40, 3.1.39 and 3.1.283), there appear to be fewer examples of this than in any other play in the Folio. The printers were evidently working from a carefully-written text. Perhaps it was a scribal copy of Shakespeare's script; perhaps it was the prompt-book or a transcript of it. Various small corrections were made to F1 during the process of printing. At what is now 5.3.97, 'haue crown'd' became 'haue not crown'd'; at 5.3.101, 'no teares' became 'mo teares'; and at the stage-direction after 5.5.23, '*Loud Alarums*' became '*Low Alarums*'.

Bearing in mind not only the principles of this Shakespeare series but also the generally high quality of the F1 text of *Julius Cæsar*, I have preserved certain of its spellings which other editors usually modernise. In this edition, therefore, you will find (for example) 'Cæsar', 'Caska', 'Calphurnia' and 'Claudio', and not 'Caesar', 'Casca', 'Calpurnia' and 'Claudius'. I also retain the occasional use of 'and' to mean 'if' and of 'tane' to mean 'taken'. The glossary explains archaisms and unfamiliar terms, while the annotations offer clarification of obscurities.

Julius Cæsar illustrates the general rule that a play by Shakespeare was initially a quantity of script-material which, in course of time, could be revised, adapted, perhaps cut, perhaps expanded, by the playwright himself and also by others, as occasion demanded. Far from being fixed and finalised, the matter was highly variable. After Shakespeare's life-time, the process of adaptation and variation continued at the hands of editors, printers, directors, players and translators.

The present edition of *Julius Cæsar* offers a practical compromise between the F1 text, Shakespeare's intentions (insofar as they can be reasonably inferred) and modern requirements. No edition of the play can claim to be definitive, but this one – aiming at clarity and concise practicality – can promise to be very useful.

THE TRAGEDY OF
JULIUS CÆSAR

CHARACTERS

JULIUS CÆSAR *and* CÆSAR'S GHOST.

CALPHURNIA, *Cæsar's wife.*

OCTAVIUS CÆSAR.
MARK ANTONY. } *Triumvirs after the death of Julius Cæsar.*
LEPIDUS.

MARCUS BRUTUS, *who joins the conspiracy.*

PORTIA, *Brutus' wife.*

LUCIUS, *Brutus' servant.*

CICERO.
PUBLIUS. } *Senators.*
POPILLIUS LENA.

CAIUS CASSIUS.
CASKA.
TREBONIUS.
CAIUS LIGARIUS. } *Conspirators against Julius Cæsar.*
DECIUS BRUTUS.
METELLUS CIMBER.
CINNA.

FLAVIUS *and* MURELLUS, *tribunes.*

A SOOTHSAYER.

ARTEMIDORUS.

CINNA *the Poet.*

Another POET.

PINDARUS, *Cassius' bondman.*

LUCILLIUS, MESSALA, VARRUS, CLAUDIO, *young* CATO,
LABIO, DARDANIUS, CLITUS, *another* FLAVIUS, STRATO, TITINIUS,
STATILLIUS *and* VOLUMNIUS, *campaigners for Brutus and Cassius.*

COBBLER, CARPENTER *and other* PLEBEIANS ('COMMONERS').

MESSENGER.

CITIZENS, SOLDIERS, BEARERS *and* SERVANTS.

Locations: Rome; the vicinity of Sardis; the plains of Philippi.

JULIUS CÆSAR[1]

ACT I, SCENE I.

Rome. A street.

Enter a CARPENTER, *a* COBBLER *and other* COMMONERS; *then enter,
approaching them,* FLAVIUS *and* MURELLUS.

FLAVIUS	Hence! Home, you idle creatures, get you home!
	Is this a holiday? What, know you not,
	Being mechanical, you ought not walk
	Upon a labouring day without the sign
	Of your profession? – Speak, what trade art thou?
CARP.	Why, sir, a carpenter.
MURELLUS	Where is thy leather apron and thy rule?
	What dost thou with thy best apparel on?
	– You, sir, what trade are you?
COBBLER	Truly, sir, in respect of a fine workman, I am but, as you 10 would say, a cobbler.[2]
MURELLUS	But what trade art thou? Answer me directly.
COBBLER	A trade, sir, that I hope I may use with a safe conscience, which is indeed, sir, a mender of bad soles.
FLAVIUS	What trade, thou knave? Thou naughty knave,
	what trade?
COBBLER	Nay, I beseech you, sir, be not out with me; yet if you be out, sir, I can mend you.
MURELLUS	What mean'st thou by that? 'Mend' me, thou
	saucy fellow?
COBBLER	Why, sir, cobble you.
FLAVIUS	Thou art a cobbler, art thou? 20
COBBLER	Truly, sir, all that I live by is with the awl: I meddle with no tradesman's matters, nor women's matters, but with awl. I am indeed, sir, a surgeon to old shoes: when they are in great danger, I recover them. As proper men as ever trod upon neat's leather have gone upon my handiwork.
FLAVIUS	But wherefore art not in thy shop today?
	Why dost thou lead these men about the streets?
COBBLER	Truly, sir, to wear out their shoes, to get myself into

more work. But indeed, sir, we make holiday to see 30
Cæsar and to rejoice in his triumph.³

MURELLUS Wherefore rejoice? What conquest brings he home?
What tributaries follow him to Rome,
To grace in captive bonds his chariot-wheels?
You blocks, you stones, you worse than senseless
                                                                    things!
O you hard hearts, you cruel men of Rome,
Knew you not Pompey?⁴ Many a time and oft
Have you climbed up to walls and battlements,
To towers and windows, yea, to chimney-tops,
Your infants in your arms, and there have sat   40
The live-long day, with patient expectation,
To see great Pompey pass the streets of Rome;
And when you saw his chariot but appear,
Have you not made an universal shout,
That Tiber trembled underneath her banks
To hear the replication of your sounds
Made in her concave shores?
And do you now put on your best attire?
And do you now cull out a holiday?
And do you now strew flowers in his way,   50
That comes in triumph over Pompey's blood?
Be gone!
Run to your houses, fall upon your knees,
Pray to the gods to intermit the plague
That needs must light on this ingratitude.

FLAVIUS Go, go, good countrymen, and for this fault
Assemble all the poor men of your sort;
Draw them to Tiber banks, and weep your tears
Into the channel, till the lowest stream
Do kiss the most exalted shores of all.   60
                              [*Exeunt all the commoners.*
See whe'r their basest mettle be not moved:
They vanish tongue-tied in their guiltiness.
Go you down that way towards the Capitol;
This way will I. Disrobe the images,
If you do find them decked with cer'monies.⁵

MURELLUS May we do so?

You know it is the Feast of Lupercal.[6]

FLAVIUS   It is no matter; let no images
Be hung with Cæsar's trophies. I'll about,
And drive away the vulgar from the streets;   70
So do you too, where you perceive them thick.
These growing feathers, plucked from Cæsar's wing,
Will make him fly an ordinary pitch,
Who else would soar above the view of men
And keep us all in servile fearfulness.

[*Exeunt.*

SCENE 2.

Music. Enter CÆSAR, ANTONY (*lightly clad for running*), CALPHURNIA,
    PORTIA, DECIUS, CICERO, BRUTUS, CASSIUS, CASKA, *a*
        SOOTHSAYER *and a crowd of* CITIZENS, *followed by*
                    MURELLUS *and* FLAVIUS.

CÆSAR   Calphurnia!
CASKA   Peace, ho! Cæsar speaks.   [*Music stops.*
CÆSAR   Calphurnia!
CALPHURN. [*coming forward:*] Here, my lord.
CÆSAR   Stand you directly in Antonio's way,
When he doth run his course. – Antonio![7]
ANTONY   Cæsar, my lord.
CÆSAR   Forget not, in your speed, Antonio,
To touch Calphurnia; for our elders say,
The barren, touchèd in this holy chase,
Shake off their sterile curse.
ANTONY   I shall remember:
When Cæsar says 'Do this', it is performed.   10
CÆSAR   Set on, and leave no ceremony out.   [*Music resumes.*
SOOTH.   Cæsar!
CÆSAR   Ha? Who calls?
CASKA   Bid every noise be still: peace yet again!   [*Music stops.*
CÆSAR   Who is it in the press that calls on me?
I hear a tongue, shriller than all the music,
Cry 'Cæsar!'. Speak, Cæsar is turned to hear.
SOOTH.   Beware the Ides of March.
CÆSAR   What man is that?

BRUTUS	A soothsayer bids you beware the Ides of March.[8]
CÆSAR	Set him before me: let me see his face.
CASSIUS	Fellow, come from the throng; look upon Cæsar.
CÆSAR	What say'st thou to me now? Speak once again.
SOOTH.	Beware the Ides of March.
CÆSAR	He is a dreamer: let us leave him. Pass!

20

      [Sennet. Exeunt all except Brutus and Cassius.

CASSIUS Will you go see the order of the course?

BRUTUS Not I.

CASSIUS I pray you, do.

BRUTUS I am not gamesome: I do lack some part
    Of that quick spirit that is in Antony.
    Let me not hinder, Cassius, your desires;
    I'll leave you.

30

CASSIUS Brutus, I do observe you now of late:
    I have not from your eyes that gentleness
    And show of love as I was wont to have:
    You bear too stubborn and too strange a hand
    Over your friend that loves you.

BRUTUS   Cassius,
    Be not deceived: if I have veiled my look,
    I turn the trouble of my countenance
    Merely upon myself. Vexèd I am
    Of late with passions of some difference,
    Conceptions only proper to myself,
    Which give some soil (perhaps) to my behaviours;
    But let not therefore my good friends be grieved
    (Among which number, Cassius, be you one),
    Nor cónstrue any further my neglect
    Than that poor Brutus, with himself at war,
    Forgets the shows of love to other men.

40

CASSIUS Then, Brutus, I have much mistook your passion,
    By means whereof this breast of mine hath buried
    Thoughts of great value, worthy cogitations.
    Tell me, good Brutus, can you see your face?

50

BRUTUS No, Cassius; for the eye sees not itself
    But by reflection, by some other things.

CASSIUS 'Tis just;
    And it is very much lamented, Brutus,

That you have no such mirrors as will turn
Your hidden worthiness into your eye,
That you might see your shadow. I have heard
Where many of the best respect in Rome
(Except immortal Cæsar), speaking of Brutus, 60
And groaning underneath this age's yoke,
Have wished that noble Brutus had his eyes.

BRUTUS   Into what dangers would you lead me, Cassius,
That you would have me seek into myself
For that which is not in me?

CASSIUS   Therefore, good Brutus, be prepared to hear;
And since you know you cannot see yourself
So well as by reflection, I, your glass,
Will modestly discover to yourself
That of yourself which you yet know not of. 70
And be not jealous on me, gentle Brutus:
Were I a common laughter, or did use
To stale with ordinary oaths my love
To every new protester; if you know
That I do fawn on men and hug them hard,
And after scandal them; or if you know
That I profess myself in banqueting
To all the rout, then hold me dangerous.
                    [*A flourish and shouting are heard.*

BRUTUS   What means this shouting? I do fear, the people
Choose Cæsar for their king.

CASSIUS   Ay, do you fear it? 80
Then must I think you would not have it so.

BRUTUS   I would not, Cassius; yet I love him well.
But wherefore do you hold me here so long?
What is it that you would impart to me?
If it be aught toward the general good,
Set honour in one eye and death i'th'other,
And I will look on both indifferently:
For let the gods so speed me as I love
The name of honour more than I fear death.

CASSIUS   I know that virtue to be in you, Brutus, 90
As well as I do know your outward favour.
Well, honour is the subject of my story.

I cannot tell what you and other men
Think of this life; but, for my single self,
I had as lief not be, as live to be
In awe of such a thing as I myself.
I was born free as Cæsar; so were you;
We both have fed as well, and we can both
Endure the winter's cold as well as he.
For once, upon a raw and gusty day,   100
The troubled Tiber chafing with her shores,
Cæsar said to me, 'Dar'st thou, Cassius, now
Leap in with me into this angry flood,
And swim to yonder point?' Upon the word,
Accoutred as I was, I plungèd in
And bade him follow: so indeed he did.
The torrent roared, and we did buffet it
With lusty sinews, throwing it aside
And stemming it with hearts of controversy.
But ere we could arrive the point proposed,   110
Cæsar cried 'Help me, Cassius, or I sink!'
Ay, as Æneas, our great ancestor,
Did from the flames of Troy upon his shoulder
The old Anchises bear, so from the waves of Tiber
Did I the tired Cæsar;[9] and this man
Is now become a god, and Cassius is
A wretched creature, and must bend his body
If Cæsar carelessly but nod on him.
He had a fever when he was in Spain,
And when the fit was on him, I did mark   120
How he did shake: 'tis true, this god did shake;[10]
His coward lips did from their colour fly,
And that same eye whose bend doth awe the world
Did lose his lustre. I did hear him groan;
Ay, and that tongue of his that bade the Romans
Mark him and write his speeches in their books,
Alas, it cried 'Give me some drink, Titinius',
As a sick girl. Ye gods! It doth amaze me,
A man of such a feeble temper should
So get the start of the majestic world,   130
And bear the palm alone. [*Shouting and a flourish are heard.*

BRUTUS	Another general shout!

I do believe that these applauses are
For some new honours that are heaped on Cæsar.

CASSIUS   Why, man, he doth bestride the narrow world
Like a Colossus,[11] and we petty men
Walk under his huge legs and peep about
To find ourselves dishonourable graves.
Men, at some time, are masters of their fates.
The fault, dear Brutus, is not in our stars,   140
But in ourselves, that we are underlings.
'Brutus' and 'Cæsar': what should be in that 'Cæsar'?
Why should that name be sounded more than yours?
Write them together: yours is as fair a name;
Sound them, it doth become the mouth as well;
Weigh them, it is as heavy; conjure with 'em,
'Brutus' will start a spirit as soon as 'Cæsar'.
Now, in the names of all the gods at once,
Upon what meat doth this our Cæsar feed,
That he is grown so great? Age, thou art shamed!   150
Rome, thou hast lost the breed of noble bloods!
When went there by an age, since the Great Flood,[12]
But it was famed with more than with one man?
When could they say, till now, that talked of Rome,
That her wide walks encompassed but one man?
Now is it Rome indeed, and room enough,[13]
When there is in it but one only man.
O, you and I have heard our fathers say
There was a Brutus once that would have brooked
Th'eternal Devil to keep his state in Rome   160
As easily as a king.[14]

BRUTUS   That you do love me, I am nothing jealous;
What you would work me to, I have some aim.
How I have thought of this and of these times,
I shall recount hereafter. For this present,
I would not so (with love I might entreat you)
Be any further moved. What you have said,
I will consider; what you have to say,
I will with patience hear, and find a time
Both meet to hear and answer such high things.   170

Till then, my noble friend, chew upon this:
Brutus had rather be a villager
Than to repute himself a son of Rome
Under these hard conditions as this time
Is like to lay upon us.

CASSIUS I am glad that my weak words
Have struck but thus much show of fire from Brutus.

Enter CÆSAR *and his* TRAIN, *including* CASKA.

BRUTUS The games are done, and Cæsar is returning.

CASSIUS As they pass by, pluck Caska by the sleeve,
And he will (after his sour fashion) tell you   180
What hath proceeded worthy note today.

BRUTUS I will do so; but, look you, Cassius,
The angry spot doth glow on Cæsar's brow,
And all the rest look like a chidden train:
Calphurnia's cheek is pale, and Cicero
Looks with such ferret and such fiery eyes[15]
As we have seen him in the Capitol,
Being crossed in conference by some senators.[16]

CASSIUS Caska will tell us what the matter is.

CÆSAR Antonio!   190

ANTONY Cæsar?

CÆSAR Let me have men about me that are fat,
Sleek-headed men, and such as sleep a-nights.
Yond Cassius has a lean and hungry look;
He thinks too much: such men are dangerous.[17]

ANTONY Fear him not, Cæsar; he's not dangerous;
He is a noble Roman, and well given.

CÆSAR Would he were fatter; but I fear him not.
Yet if my name were liable to fear,
I do not know the man I should avoid   200
So soon as that spare Cassius. He reads much;
He is a great observer, and he looks
Quite through the deeds of men. He loves no plays,
As thou dost, Antony; he hears no music;
Seldom he smiles, and smiles in such a sort
As if he mocked himself and scorned his spirit
That could be moved to smile at any thing.
Such men as he be never at heart's ease

Whiles they behold a greater than themselves,
And therefore are they very dangerous.   210
I rather tell thee what is to be feared,
Than what I fear; for always I am Cæsar.
Come on my right hand, for this ear is deaf,[18]
And tell me truly what thou think'st of him.

[*Sennet. Exeunt Cæsar and his train, but Caska remains.*

CASKA	You pulled me by the cloak: would you speak with me?
BRUTUS	Ay, Caska; tell us what hath chanced today,
	That Cæsar looks so sad.
CASKA	Why, you were with him, were you not?
BRUTUS	I should not then ask Caska what had chanced.
CASKA	Why, there was a crown offered him; and being offered 220
	him, he put it by with the back of his hand, thus; and
	then the people fell a-shouting.[19]
BRUTUS	What was the second noise for?
CASKA	Why, for that too.
CASSIUS	They shouted thrice: what was the last cry for?
CASKA	Why, for that too.
BRUTUS	Was the crown offered him thrice?
caska	Ay, marry, was't, and he put it by thrice, every time
	gentler than other; and, at every putting-by, mine hon-
	est neighbours shouted. 230
CASSIUS	Who offered him the crown?
CASKA	Why, Antony.
BRUTUS	Tell us the manner of it, gentle Caska.
CASKA	I can as well be hanged as tell the manner of it: it was

mere foolery; I did not mark it. I saw Mark Antony offer
him a crown, yet 'twas not a crown neither, 'twas one of
these coronets; and, as I told you, he put it by once; but
for all that, to my thinking, he would fain have had it.
Then he offered it to him again; then he put it by again;
but, to my thinking, he was very loath to lay his fingers
off it. And then he offered it the third time; he put it the 240
third time by; and still as he refused it, the rabblement
hooted, and clapped their chopped hands, and threw up
their sweaty night-caps, and uttered such a deal of stink-
ing breath, because Cæsar refused the crown, that it had
(almost) choked Cæsar; for he swoonded and fell down

at it; and for mine own part, I durst not laugh, for fear of
opening my lips and receiving the bad air.

CASSIUS   But, soft, I pray you: what, did Cæsar swoond?

CASKA   He fell down in the market-place, and foamed at mouth,
           and was speechless.   250

BRUTUS   'Tis very like: he hath the falling sickness.

CASSIUS   No, Cæsar hath it not; but you, and I,
           And honest Caska, we have the falling sickness.

CASKA   I know not what you mean by that, but I am sure Cæsar
           fell down. If the tag-rag people did not clap him and
           hiss him, according as he pleased and displeased them, as
           they use to do the players in the theatre, I am no true
           man.

BRUTUS   What said he, when he came unto himself?

CASKA   Marry, before he fell down, when he perceived the   260
           common herd was glad he refused the crown, he plucked
           me ope his doublet, and offered them his throat to cut.[20]
           And I had been a man of any occupation, if I would not
           have taken him at a word, I would I might go to Hell
           among the rogues. And so he fell. When he came to
           himself again, he said, if he had done or said anything
           amiss, he desired their worships to think it was his
           infirmity. Three or four wenches, where I stood, cried
           'Alas, good soul!' and forgave him with all their hearts;
           but there's no heed to be taken of them: if Cæsar had   270
           stabbed their mothers, they would have done no less.

BRUTUS   And after that, he came, thus sad, away.

CASKA   Ay.

CASSIUS   Did Cicero say anything?

CASKA   Ay, he spoke Greek.

CASSIUS   To what effect?

CASKA   Nay, and I tell you that, I'll ne'er look you i'th'face again.
           But those that understood him smiled at one another
           and shook their heads; but for mine own part, it was
           Greek to me. I could tell you more news too: Murellus   280
           and Flavius, for pulling scarves off Cæsar's images, are
           put to silence.[21] Fare you well. There was more foolery
           yet, if I could remember it.

CASSIUS   Will you sup with me tonight, Caska?

CASKA   No, I am promised forth.

CASSIUS   Will you dine with me tomorrow?

CASKA   Ay, if I be alive, and your mind hold, and your dinner
worth the eating.

CASSIUS   Good; I will expect you.

CASKA   Do so; farewell both.   [*Exit.* 290

BRUTUS   What a blunt fellow is this grown to be!
He was quick mettle when he went to school.

CASSIUS   So is he now, in execution
Of any bold or noble enterprise,
However he puts on this tardy form.
This rudeness is a sauce to his good wit,
Which gives men stomach to digest his words
With better appetite.

BRUTUS   And so it is. For this time I will leave you.
Tomorrow, if you please to speak with me,   300
I will come home to you; or, if you will,
Come home to me, and I will wait for you.

CASSIUS   I will do so; till then, think of the world. [*Exit Brutus.*
Well, Brutus, thou art noble; yet I see,
Thy honourable mettle may be wrought
From that it is disposed: therefore it is meet
That noble minds keep ever with their likes;
For who so firm that cannot be seduced?
Cæsar doth bear me hard, but he loves Brutus.
If I were Brutus now, and he were Cassius,   310
He should not humour me. I will this night,
In several hands, in at his windows throw
– As if they came from several citizens –
Writings,[22] all tending to the great opinion
That Rome holds of his name, wherein obscurely
Cæsar's ambition shall be glanced at.[23]
And after this, let Cæsar seat him sure,
For we will shake him, or worse days endure.
                                   [*Exit.*

SCENE 3.

A street. Midnight.

Thunder and lightning. Enter, from different directions,
CASKA, with his sword drawn, and CICERO.

CICERO Good even, Caska: brought you Cæsar home?
Why are you breathless? And why stare you so?

CASKA Are not you moved, when all the sway of earth
Shakes like a thing unfirm? O Cicero,
I have seen tempests, when the scolding winds
Have rived the knotty oaks, and I have seen
Th'ambitious ocean swell, and rage, and foam,
To be exalted with the threat'ning clouds;
But never till tonight, never till now,
Did I go through a tempest dropping fire.   10
Either there is a civil strife in Heaven,
Or else the world, too saucy with the gods,
Incenses them to send destruction.

CICERO Why, saw you any thing more wonderful?

CASKA A common slave – you know him well by sight –
Held up his left hand, which did flame and burn
Like twenty torches joined; and yet his hand,
Not sensible of fire, remained unscorched.[24]
Besides – I ha' not since put up my sword –
Against the Capitol I met a lion,   20
Who glazed upon me and went surly by
Without annoying me. And there were drawn
Upon a heap a hundred ghastly women,
Transformèd with their fear, who swore they saw
Men all in fire walk up and down the streets.
And yesterday, the bird of night did sit
Even at noon-day upon the market-place,
Hooting and shrieking.[25] When these prodigies
Do so conjointly meet, let not men say
'These are their reasons, they are natural';   30
For, I believe, they are portentous things
Unto the climate that they point upon.

CICERO	Indeed, it is a strange-disposèd time;
	But men may cónstrue things after their fashion,
	Clean from the purpose of the things themselves.
	Comes Cæsar to the Capitol tomorrow?
CASKA	He doth; for he did bid Antonio
	Send word to you he would be there tomorrow.
CICERO	Good night then, Caska: this disturbèd sky
	Is not to walk in.
CASKA	Farewell, Cicero. [*Exit Cicero.* 40

Enter CASSIUS, *jacket open.*

CASSIUS	Who's there?
CASKA	A Roman.
CASSIUS	Caska, by your voice.
CASKA	Your ear is good. Cassius, what night is this?
CASSIUS	A very pleasing night to honest men.
CASKA	Who ever knew the heavens menace so?
CASSIUS	Those that have known the earth so full of faults.
	For my part, I have walked about the streets,
	Submitting me unto the perilous night;
	And thus unbracèd, Caska, as you see,
	Have bared my bosom to the thunder-stone;
	And when the cross blue lightning seemed to open 50
	The breast of heaven, I did present myself
	Even in the aim and very flash of it.
CASKA	But wherefore did you so much tempt the heavens?
	It is the part of men to fear and tremble
	When the most mighty gods by tokens send
	Such dreadful heralds to astonish us.
CASSIUS	You are dull, Caska, and those sparks of life
	That should be in a Roman you do want,
	Or else you use not. You look pale, and gaze,
	And put on fear, and cast yourself in wonder, 60
	To see the strange impatience of the heavens;
	But if you would consider the true cause,
	Why all these fires, why all these gliding ghosts,
	Why birds and beasts from quality and kind,
	Why old men, fools and children calculate,
	Why all these things change from their ordinance,
	Their natures and preformèd faculties,

    To monstrous quality: why, you shall find
    That heaven hath infused them with these spirits
    To make them instruments of fear and warning   70
    Unto some monstrous state.
    Now could I, Caska, name to thee a man
    Most like this dreadful night,
    That thunders, lightens, opens graves, and roars
    As doth the lion in the Capitol;
    A man no mightier than thyself or me
    In personal action, yet prodigious grown
    And fearful, as these strange eruptions are.

CASKA   'Tis Cæsar that you mean; is it not, Cassius?

CASSIUS   Let it be who it is; for Romans now   80
    Have thews and limbs like to their ancestors',
    But, woe the while, our fathers' minds are dead,
    And we are governed with our mothers' spirits:
    Our yoke and sufferance show us womanish.

CASKA   Indeed, they say the senators tomorrow
    Mean to establish Cæsar as a king;
    And he shall wear his crown by sea and land,
    In every place save here in Italy.

CASSIUS   I know where I will wear this dagger then:
    Cassius from bondage will deliver Cassius.   90
    Therein, ye gods, you make the weak most strong;
    Therein, ye gods, you tyrants do defeat.
    Nor stony tower, nor walls of beaten brass,
    Nor airless dungeon, nor strong links of iron,
    Can be retentive to the strength of spirit;
    But life, being weary of these worldly bars,
    Never lacks power to dismiss itself.
    If I know this, know all the world besides,
    That part of tyranny that I do bear,
    I can shake off at pleasure.   [*Thunder continues.*

CASKA   So can I;   100
    So every bondman in his own hand bears
    The power to cancel his captivity.

CASSIUS   And why should Cæsar be a tyrant then?
    Poor man! I know he would not be a wolf,
    But that he sees the Romans are but sheep:

He were no lion, were not Romans hinds.
Those that with haste will make a mighty fire
Begin it with weak straws. What trash is Rome,
What rubbish and what offal, when it serves
For the base matter to illuminate   110
So vile a thing as Cæsar! But, O grief,
Where hast thou led me? I (perhaps) speak this
Before a willing bondman; then I know
My answer must be made. But I am armed,
And dangers are to me indifferent.

CASKA   You speak to Caska, and to such a man
That is no fleering tell-tale. Hold; my hand.
Be factious for redress of all these griefs,
And I will set this foot of mine as far
As who goes farthest.   [They clasp hands.

CASSIUS   There's a bargain made.   120
Now know you, Caska, I have moved already
Some certain of the noblest-minded Romans
To undergo with me an enterprise
Of honourable dangerous consequence;
And I do know, by this they stay for me
In Pompey's Porch;[26] for now, this fearful night,
There is no stir or walking in the streets,
And the complexion of the element
In favour's like the work we have in hand,[27]
Most bloody, fiery, and most terrible.   130

Enter CINNA.

CASKA   Stand close a while, for here comes one in haste.
CASSIUS 'Tis Cinna; I do know him by his gait;
He is a friend. – Cinna, where haste you so?
CINNA   To find out you. Who's that? Metellus Cimber?
CASSIUS No, it is Caska, one incorporate
To our attempts. Am I not stayed for, Cinna?
CINNA   I am glad on't. What a fearful night is this!
There's two or three of us have seen strange sights.
CASSIUS Am I not stayed for? Tell me.
CINNA   Yes, you are.
O Cassius, if you could   140
But win the noble Brutus to our party –

CASSIUS   Be you content. Good Cinna, take this paper,
           And look you lay it in the prætor's chair,
           Where Brutus may but find it; and throw this
           In at his window; set this up with wax
           Upon old Brutus' statue;[28] all this done,
           Repair to Pompey's Porch, where you shall find us.
           Is Decius Brutus and Trebonius there?
CINNA   All but Metellus Cimber, and he's gone
           To seek you at your house. Well, I will hie,   150
           And so bestow these papers as you bade me.
CASSIUS   That done, repair to Pompey's Theatre.[29] [*Exit Cinna.*
           Come, Caska, you and I will yet, ere day,
           See Brutus at his house: three parts of him
           Is ours already, and the man entire
           Upon the next encounter yields him ours.
CASKA   O, he sits high in all the people's hearts;
           And that which would appear offence in us,
           His countenance, like richest alchemy,
           Will change to virtue and to worthiness.   160
CASSIUS   Him and his worth, and our great need of him,
           You have right well conceited. Let us go,
           For it is after midnight; and, ere day,
           We will awake him and be sure of him.

                                                    [*Exeunt.*

ACT 2, SCENE 1.

Brutus' orchard.

Enter BRUTUS.

BRUTUS What, Lucius, ho!
    – I cannot, by the progress of the stars,
    Give guess how near to day. – Lucius, I say! –
    I would it were my fault to sleep so soundly.
    – When, Lucius, when? Awake, I say! What, Lucius!

Enter LUCIUS.

LUCIUS Called you, my lord?
BRUTUS Get me a taper in my study, Lucius:
    When it is lighted, come and call me here.
LUCIUS I will, my lord.   [*Exit.*
BRUTUS It must be by his death; and, for my part,   10
    I know no personal cause to spurn at him,
    But for the general. He would be crowned:
    How that might change his nature, there's the question.
    It is the bright day that brings forth the adder,
    And that craves wary walking. Crown him, that,
    And then I grant we put a sting in him,
    That at his will he may do danger with.
    Th'abuse of greatness is when it disjoins
    Remorse from power; and, to speak truth of Cæsar,
    I have not known when his affections swayed   20
    More than his reason. But 'tis a common proof,
    That lowliness is young ambition's ladder,
    Whereto the climber upward turns his face;
    But when he once attains the upmost round,
    He then unto the ladder turns his back,
    Looks in the clouds, scorning the base degrees
    By which he did ascend: so Cæsar may;
    Then, lest he may, prevent. And, since the quarrel
    Will bear no colour for the thing he is,
    Fashion it thus: that what he is, augmented,   30
    Would run to these and these extremities;

And therefore think him as a serpent's egg
(Which, hatched, would as his kind grow mischievous),
And kill him in the shell.

Enter LUCIUS.

LUCIUS   The taper burneth in your closet, sir.
Searching the window for a flint, I found
This paper, thus sealed up; and I am sure
It did not lie there when I went to bed.

[Lucius gives him the letter.

BRUTUS   Get you to bed again; it is not day.
Is not tomorrow, boy, the Ides of March?[30]   40

LUCIUS   I know not, sir.

BRUTUS   Look in the calendar and bring me word.

LUCIUS   I will, sir.   *[Exit.*

BRUTUS   The exhalations whizzing in the air
Give so much light that I may read by them.

[He opens the letter and reads.

'Brutus, thou sleep'st: awake and see thyself.
Shall Rome, et cetera? Speak, strike, redress.' –
'Brutus, thou sleep'st: awake':
Such instigations have been often dropped
Where I have took them up.   50
'Shall Rome, et cetera?' Thus must I piece it out:
Shall Rome stand under one man's awe? What, Rome?
My ancestors did from the streets of Rome
The Tarquin drive, when he was called a king.
'Speak, strike, redress.' Am I entreated
To speak and strike? O Rome, I make thee promise,
If the redress will follow, thou receivest
Thy full petition at the hand of Brutus.

Enter LUCIUS.

LUCIUS   Sir, March is wasted fifteen days.   *[Knocking heard.*

BRUTUS   'Tis good. Go to the gate; somebody knocks.   60

[Exit Lucius.

Since Cassius first did whet me against Cæsar,
I have not slept.
Between the acting of a dreadful thing
And the first motion, all the interim is

Like a phantasma or a hideous dream:
The genius and the mortal instruments
Are then in council; and the state of man,[31]
Like to a little kingdom, suffers then
The nature of an insurrection.

Enter LUCIUS.

LUCIUS   Sir, 'tis your brother Cassius[32] at the door,   70
   Who doth desire to see you.
BRUTUS   Is he alone?
LUCIUS   No, sir, there are moe with him.
BRUTUS   Do you know them?
LUCIUS   No, sir, their hats are plucked about their ears,[33]
   And half their faces buried in their cloaks,
   That by no means I may discover them
   By any mark of favour.
BRUTUS   Let 'em enter. [*Exit Lucius.*
   They are the faction. O conspiracy,
   Sham'st thou to show thy dang'rous brow by night,
   When evils are most free? O then, by day,
   Where wilt thou find a cavern dark enough   80
   To mask thy monstrous visage? Seek none, conspiracy;
   Hide it in smiles and affability:
   For if thou path, thy native semblance on,[34]
   Not Erebus itself were dim enough
   To hide thee from prevention.

Enter the conspirators, CASSIUS, CASKA, DECIUS, CINNA,
METELLUS *and* TREBONIUS.

CASSIUS   I think we are too bold upon your rest.
   Good morrow, Brutus; do we trouble you?
BRUTUS   I have been up this hour, awake all night.
   Know I these men that come along with you?
CASSIUS   Yes, every man of them; and no man here   90
   But honours you; and every one doth wish
   You had but that opinion of yourself
   Which every noble Roman bears of you.
   This is Trebonius.
BRUTUS   He is welcome hither.
CASSIUS   This, Decius Brutus.

BRUTUS	He is welcome too.
CASSIUS	This, Caska; this, Cinna; and this, Metellus Cimber.
BRUTUS	They are all welcome.
	What watchful cares do interpose themselves
	Betwixt your eyes and night?
CASSIUS	Shall I entreat a word? [*The two whisper privately.* 100
DECIUS	Here lies the east: doth not the day break here?
CASKA	No.
CINNA	O pardon, sir, it doth; and yon grey lines
	That fret the clouds are messengers of day.
CASKA	You shall confess that you are both deceived.
	Here, as I point my sword, the sun arises;
	Which is a great way growing on the south,
	Weighing the youthful season of the year.
	Some two months hence, up higher toward the north
	He first presents his fire, and the high east 110
	Stands as the Capitol, directly here.

                           [*Brutus and Cassius rejoin the group.*

BRUTUS	Give me your hands all over, one by one –
CASSIUS	And let us swear our resolution.
BRUTUS	No, not an oath. If not the face of men,
	The sufferance of our souls, the time's abuse –
	If these be motives weak, break off betimes,
	And every man hence to his idle bed.
	So let high-sighted tyranny range on
	Till each man drop by lottery. But if these
	(As I am sure they do) bear fire enough 120
	To kindle cowards and to steel with valour
	The melting spirits of women, then, countrymen,
	What need we any spur but our own cause
	To prick us to redress? What other bond
	Than secret Romans that have spoke the word,
	And will not palter? And what other oath
	Than honesty to honesty engaged,
	That this shall be or we will fall for it?
	Swear priests and cowards and men cautelous,
	Old feeble carrions, and such suffering souls 130
	That welcome wrongs. Unto bad causes swear
	Such creatures as men doubt; but do not stain

	The even virtue of our enterprise,	
	Nor th'insuppressive mettle of our spirits,	
	To think that or our cause or our performance	
	Did need an oath, when every drop of blood	
	That every Roman bears, and nobly bears,	
	Is guilty of a several bastardy	
	If he do break the smallest particle	
	Of any promise that hath passed from him.	140
CASSIUS	But what of Cicero? Shall we sound him?	
	I think he will stand very strong with us.	
CASKA	Let us not leave him out.	
CINNA	No, by no means.	
METELLUS	O, let us have him, for his silver hairs	
	Will purchase us a good opinion	
	And buy men's voices to commend our deeds:	
	It shall be said, his judgement ruled our hands;	
	Our youths and wildness shall no whit appear,	
	But all be buried in his gravity.	
BRUTUS	O name him not; let us not break with him,	150
	For he will never follow any thing	
	That other men begin.	
CASSIUS	Then leave him out.	
CASKA	Indeed he is not fit.	
DECIUS	Shall no man else be touched, but only Cæsar?	
CASSIUS	Decius, well urged. I think it is not meet	
	Mark Antony, so well beloved of Cæsar,	
	Should outlive Cæsar: we shall find of him	
	A shrewd contriver; and you know, his means,	
	If he improve them, may well stretch so far	
	As to annoy us all: which to prevent,	160
	Let Antony and Cæsar fall together.	
BRUTUS	Our course will seem too bloody, Caius Cassius,	
	To cut the head off and then hack the limbs,	
	Like wrath in death and envy afterwards;	
	For Antony is but a limb of Cæsar.	
	Let's be sacrificers, but not butchers, Caius.[35]	
	We all stand up against the spirit of Cæsar,	
	And in the spirit of men there is no blood:	
	O, that we then could come by Cæsar's spirit,	

| | And not dismember Cæsar! But, alas, | 170 |

And not dismember Cæsar! But, alas,   170
Cæsar must bleed for it. And, gentle friends,
Let's kill him boldly, but not wrathfully:
Let's carve him as a dish fit for the gods,
Not hew him as a carcass fit for hounds;
And let our hearts, as subtle masters do,
Stir up their servants to an act of rage
And after seem to chide 'em. This shall make
Our purpose necessary, and not envious;
Which so appearing to the common eyes,
We shall be called purgers, not murderers.   180
And for Mark Antony, think not of him;
For he can do no more than Cæsar's arm
When Cæsar's head is off.

CASSIUS   Yet I fear him,
For in the ingrafted love he bears to Cæsar –

BRUTUS   Alas, good Cassius, do not think of him.
If he love Cæsar, all that he can do
Is to himself: take thought, and die for Cæsar;
And that were much he should, for he is given
To sports, to wildness and much company.

TREBON.   There is no fear in him;[36] let him not die;   190
For he will live and laugh at this hereafter.
                              [*A clock strikes.*[37]

BRUTUS   Peace; count the clock.

CASSIUS   The clock hath stricken three.

TREBON.   'Tis time to part.

CASSIUS   But it is doubtful yet
Whether Cæsar will come forth today or no;
For he is superstitious grown of late,
Quite from the main opinion he held once
Of fantasy, of dreams and cer'monies.
It may be, these apparent prodigies,
The unaccustomed terror of this night,
And the persuasion of his augurers,   200
May hold him from the Capitol today.

DECIUS   Never fear that: if he be so resolved,
I can o'ersway him; for he loves to hear
That unicorns may be betrayed with trees,

And bears with glasses, elephants with holes,
Lions with toils,[38] and men with flatterers;
But when I tell him he hates flatterers,
He says he does, being then most flatterèd.
Let me work;
For I can give his humour the true bent,   210
And I will bring him to the Capitol.

CASSIUS   Nay, we will all of us be there to fetch him.

BRUTUS   By the eighth hour: is that the uttermost?

CINNA   Be that the uttermost, and fail not then.

METELLUS   Caius Ligarius doth bear Cæsar hard,
Who rated him for speaking well of Pompey:
I wonder none of you have thought of him.

BRUTUS   Now, good Metellus, go along by him:
He loves me well, and I have given him reasons;
Send him but hither, and I'll fashion him.   220

CASSIUS   The morning comes upon's: we'll leave you, Brutus;
And, friends, disperse yourselves; but all remember
What you have said, and show yourselves true Romans.

BRUTUS   Good gentlemen, look fresh and merrily;
Let not our looks put on our purposes,
But bear it as our Roman actors do,
With untired spirits and formal constancy;[39]
And so, good morrow to you every one.

                           [*Exeunt all but Brutus.*

Boy! Lucius! Fast asleep? It is no matter.
Enjoy the honey-heavy dew of slumber.   230
Thou hast no figures nor no fantasies,
Which busy care draws in the brains of men;
Therefore thou sleep'st so sound.

                 Enter PORTIA.

PORTIA   Brutus, my lord.

BRUTUS   Portia, what mean you? Wherefore rise you now?
It is not for your health, thus to commit
Your weak condition to the raw cold morning.

PORTIA   Nor for yours neither. Y'have ungently, Brutus,
Stole from my bed; and yesternight at supper
You suddenly arose, and walked about,
Musing and sighing, with your arms across;   240

And when I asked you what the matter was,
You stared upon me with ungentle looks.
I urged you further; then you scratched your head,
And too impatiently stamped with your foot.
Yet I insisted, yet you answered not,
But with an angry wafter of your hand
Gave sign for me to leave you: so I did,
Fearing to strengthen that impatience
Which seemed too much enkindled, and, withal,
Hoping it was but an effect of humour,   250
Which sometime hath his hour with every man.
It will not let you eat, nor talk, nor sleep,
And, could it work so much upon your shape
As it hath much prevailed on your condition,
I should not know you Brutus.[40] Dear my lord,
Make me acquainted with your cause of grief.

BRUTUS   I am not well in health, and that is all.

PORTIA   Brutus is wise, and, were he not in health,
            He would embrace the means to come by it.

BRUTUS   Why, so I do. Good Portia, go to bed.   260

PORTIA   Is Brutus sick, and is it physical
            To walk unbracèd and suck up the humours[41]
            Of the dank morning? What, is Brutus sick,
            And will he steal out of his wholesome bed,
            To dare the vile contagion of the night,
            And tempt the rheumy and unpurgèd air
            To add unto his sickness? No, my Brutus;
            You have some sick offence within your mind,
            Which by the right and virtue of my place
            I ought to know of. [*She kneels.*] And, upon my knees,   270
            I charm you, by my once commended beauty,
            By all your vows of love, and that great vow
            Which did incorporate and make us one,
            That you unfold to me, your self, your half,
            Why you are heavy – and what men tonight
            Have had resort to you, for here have been
            Some six or seven, who did hide their faces
            Even from darkness.

BRUTUS   Kneel not, gentle Portia.

PORTIA   [*rises.*] I should not need, if you were gentle Brutus.
Within the bond of marriage, tell me, Brutus,   280
Is it excepted I should know no secrets
That appertain to you? Am I your self
But, as it were, in sort or limitation,[42]
To keep with you at meals, comfort your bed,
And talk to you sometimes? Dwell I but in the suburbs
Of your good pleasure? If it be no more,
Portia is Brutus' harlot, not his wife.

BRUTUS   You are my true and honourable wife,
As dear to me as are the ruddy drops
That visit my sad heart.   290

PORTIA   If this were true, then should I know this secret.
I grant I am a woman, but, withal,
A woman that Lord Brutus took to wife.
I grant I am a woman, but, withal,
A woman well reputed, Cato's daughter.[43]
Think you, I am no stronger than my sex,
Being so fathered and so husbanded?
Tell me your counsels; I will not disclose 'em.
I have made strong proof of my constancy,
Giving myself a voluntary wound   300
Here, in the thigh:[44] can I bear that with patience,
And not my husband's secrets?

BRUTUS   O ye gods!
Render me worthy of this noble wife!   [*Knocking heard.*
Hark, hark: one knocks. Portia, go in awhile,
And by and by thy bosom shall partake
The secrets of my heart.
All my engagements I will cónstrue to thee,
All the charáctery of my sad brows.
Leave me with haste. [*Exit Portia.*]
                 Lucius, who's that knocks?

Enter LUCIUS, *followed by* LIGARIUS, *a kerchief on his head.*[45]

LUCIUS   Here is a sick man that would speak with you.   310

BRUTUS   Caius Ligarius, that Metellus spake of.
   – Boy, stand aside. – Caius Ligarius, how?

LIGARIUS   Vouchsafe good-morrow from a feeble tongue.

BRUTUS   O, what a time have you chose out, brave Caius,

To wear a kerchief! Would you were not sick.

LIGARIUS   I am not sick, if Brutus have in hand
           Any exploit worthy the name of honour.

BRUTUS   Such an exploit have I in hand, Ligarius,
           Had you a healthful ear to hear of it.

LIGARIUS   By all the gods that Romans bow before,   320
           I here discard my sickness! [*He discards the kerchief.*]
                                        Soul of Rome!
           Brave son, derived from honourable loins,
           Thou, like an exorcist, hast conjured up
           My mortifièd spirit.[46] Now bid me run,
           And I will strive with things impossible,
           Yea, get the better of them. What's to do?

BRUTUS   A piece of work that will make sick men whole.

LIGARIUS   But are not some whole that we must make sick?

BRUTUS   That must we also. What it is, my Caius,
           I shall unfold to thee, as we are going   330
           To whom it must be done.

LIGARIUS   Set on your foot,
           And with a heart new-fired I follow you,
           To do I know not what; but it sufficeth
           That Brutus leads me on.   [*Thunder heard.*]

BRUTUS   Follow me then.
                                              [*Exeunt.*]

SCENE 2.

In Cæsar's house.

Thunder and lightning. Enter JULIUS CÆSAR, *in his dressing-gown.*

CÆSAR   Nor heaven nor earth have been at peace tonight:
    Thrice hath Calphurnia in her sleep cried out
    'Help, ho! They murther Cæsar!' [*He calls:*]
                         Who's within?

Enter a SERVANT.

SERVANT   My lord?
CÆSAR   Go bid the priests do present sacrifice,
    And bring me their opinions of success.
SERVANT   I will, my lord.   [*Exit.*

Enter CALPHURNIA.

CALPHURN. What mean you, Cæsar? Think you to walk forth?
    You shall not stir out of your house today.
CÆSAR   Cæsar shall forth: the things that threatened me   10
    Ne'er looked but on my back: when they shall see
    The face of Cæsar, they are vanishèd.
CALPHURN. Cæsar, I never stood on cer'monies,
    Yet now they fright me. There is one within,
    Besides the things that we have heard and seen,
    Recounts most horrid sights seen by the watch.
    A lioness hath whelpèd in the streets,
    And graves have yawned and yielded up their dead;
    Fierce fiery warriors fought upon the clouds,
    In ranks and squadrons and right form of war,   20
    Which drizzled blood upon the Capitol.
    The noise of battle hurtled in the air,
    Horses did neigh, and dying men did groan,
    And ghosts did shriek and squeal about the streets.[47]
    O Cæsar, these things are beyond all use,
    And I do fear them.
CÆSAR   What can be avoided,
    Whose end is purposed by the mighty gods?
    Yet Cæsar shall go forth; for these predictions

Are to the world in general as to Cæsar.

CALPHURN. When beggars die, there are no comets seen;   30
The heavens themselves blaze forth the death of princes.

CÆSAR   Cowards die many times before their deaths;
The valiant never taste of death but once.
Of all the wonders that I yet have heard,
It seems to me most strange that men should fear,[48]
Seeing that death, a necessary end,
Will come when it will come.

Enter the SERVANT.

What say the augurers?

SERVANT They would not have you to stir forth today.
Plucking the entrails of an offering forth,
They could not find a heart within the beast.   40

CÆSAR   The gods do this in shame of cowardice:
Cæsar should be a beast without a heart
If he should stay at home today for fear.
No, Cæsar shall not: Danger knows full well
That Cæsar is more dangerous than he.
We are two lions littered in one day,[49]
And I the elder and more terrible;
And Cæsar shall go forth.

CALPHURN.   Alas, my lord,
Your wisdom is consumed in confidence.
Do not go forth today: call it my fear   50
That keeps you in the house, and not your own.
We'll send Mark Antony to the Senate House,
And he shall say you are not well today.
Let me, upon my knee, prevail in this.   [*She kneels.*

CÆSAR   Mark Antony shall say I am not well,
And, for thy humour, I will stay at home.   [*She rises.*

Enter DECIUS.

Here's Decius Brutus: he shall tell them so.

DECIUS   Cæsar, all hail! Good morrow, worthy Cæsar:
I come to fetch you to the Senate House.

CÆSAR   And you are come in very happy time,   60
To bear my greeting to the senators
And tell them that I will not come today.

Cannot, is false; and that I dare not, falser.
I will not come today: tell them so, Decius.

CALPHURN. Say he is sick.

CÆSAR   Shall Cæsar send a lie?
Have I in conquest stretched mine arm so far,
To be afeard to tell greybeards the truth?
Decius, go tell them, Cæsar will not come.

DECIUS Most mighty Cæsar, let me know some cause,
Lest I be laughed at when I tell them so.   70

CÆSAR The cause is in my will: I *will* not come;
That is enough to satisfy the Senate.
But, for your private satisfaction,
Because I love you, I will let you know.
Calphurnia here, my wife, stays me at home:
She dreamt tonight she saw my statua,[50]
Which, like a fountain with an hundred spouts,
Did run pure blood, and many lusty Romans
Came smiling and did bathe their hands in it:
And these does she apply for warnings and portents   80
And evils imminent; and on her knee
Hath begged that I will stay at home today.

DECIUS This dream is all amiss interpreted;
It was a vision fair and fortunate:
Your statue spouting blood in many pipes,
In which so many smiling Romans bathed,
Signifies that from you great Rome shall suck
Reviving blood, and that great men shall press
For tinctures, stains, relíques, and cognisance.[51]
This by Calphurnia's dream is signified.   90

CÆSAR And this way have you well expounded it.

DECIUS I have, when you have heard what I can say;
And know it now: the Senate have concluded
To give this day a crown to mighty Cæsar.
If you shall send them word you will not come,
Their minds may change. Besides, it were a mock
Apt to be rendered, for some one to say[52]
'Break up the Senate till another time,
When Cæsar's wife shall meet with better dreams'.[53]
If Cæsar hide himself, shall they not whisper   100

            'Lo, Cæsar is afraid'?
            Pardon me, Cæsar; for my dear dear love
            To your proceeding bids me tell you this,
            And reason to my love is liable.

CÆSAR   How foolish do your fears seem now, Calphurnia!
            I am ashamèd I did yield to them.
            Give me my robe, for I will go.

     Enter PUBLIUS, BRUTUS, LIGARIUS, METELLUS, CASKA,
               TREBONIUS *and* CINNA.[54]

            And look where Publius is come to fetch me.
PUBLIUS   Good morrow, Cæsar.
CÆSAR   Welcome, Publius.
            – What, Brutus, are you stirred so early too?   110
            – Good morrow, Caska. – Caius Ligarius,
            Cæsar was ne'er so much your enemy
            As that same ague which hath made you lean.
            What is't o'clock?
BRUTUS   Cæsar, 'tis strucken eight.
CÆSAR   I thank you for your pains and courtesy.

                Enter ANTONY.

            See: Antony, that revels long a-nights,
            Is notwithstanding up. – Good morrow, Antony.
ANTONY   So to most noble Cæsar.
CÆSAR   [*to Calphurnia:*]   Bid them prepare within:
            I am to blame to be thus waited for.   [*Exit Calphurnia.*
            Now, Cinna, – now, Metellus; – what, Trebonius: 120
            I have an hour's talk in store for you;
            Remember that you call on me today:
            Be near me, that I may remember you.
TREBON.   Cæsar, I will. [*Aside:*] And so near will I be,
            That your best friends shall wish I had been further.
CÆSAR   Good friends, go in and taste some wine with me;
            And we, like friends, will straightway go together.
BRUTUS   [*Aside:*] That every 'like' is not the same,[55] O Cæsar,
            The heart of Brutus earns to think upon.
                             [*Exeunt.*

SCENE 3.

A street near the Capitol.

Enter ARTEMIDORUS, *reading a paper.*

ARTEM. 'Cæsar, beware of Brutus; take heed of Cassius; come
not near Caska; have an eye to Cinna; trust not
Trebonius; mark well Metellus Cimber; Decius Brutus
loves thee not; thou hast wronged Caius Ligarius.
There is but one mind in all these men, and it is bent
against Cæsar. If thou beest not immortal, look about
you: security gives way to conspiracy.[56] The mighty
gods defend thee!   Thy lover, Artemidorus.'

Here will I stand till Cæsar pass along,
And as a suitor will I give him this.   10
My heart laments that virtue cannot live
Out of the teeth of emulation.
If thou read this, O Cæsar, thou mayst live;
If not, the Fates with traitors do contrive.

            [*Exit.*

SCENE 4.

Enter PORTIA *and* LUCIUS *from Brutus' house.*

PORTIA   I prithee, boy, run to the Senate House;
Stay not to answer me, but get thee gone.
Why dost thou stay?

LUCIUS   To know my errand, madam.

PORTIUS   I would have had thee there and here again,
Ere I can tell thee what thou shouldst do there.
[*Aside:*] O constancy, be strong upon my side;
Set a huge mountain 'tween my heart and tongue.
I have a man's mind, but a woman's might.
How hard it is for women to keep counsel!
– Art thou here yet?

LUCIUS   Madam, what should I do?   10
Run to the Capitol, and nothing else?
And so return to you, and nothing else?

PORTIA	Yes, bring me word, boy, if thy lord look well,
	For he went sickly forth; and take good note
	What Cæsar doth, what suitors press to him.
	Hark, boy: what noise is that?
LUCIUS	I hear none, madam.
PORTIA	Prithee, listen well:
	I heard a bustling rumour like a fray,[57]
	And the wind brings it from the Capitol.
LUCIUS	Sooth, madam, I hear nothing.

Enter the SOOTHSAYER.

PORTIA	Come hither, fellow: 20
	Which way hast thou been?
SOOTH.	At mine own house, good lady.
PORTIA	What is't o'clock?
SOOTH.	About the ninth hour, lady.
PORTIA	Is Cæsar yet gone to the Capitol?
SOOTH.	Madam, not yet: I go to take my stand,
	To see him pass on to the Capitol.
PORTIA	Thou hast some suit to Cæsar, hast thou not?
SOOTH.	That I have, lady: if it will please Cæsar
	To be so good to Cæsar as to hear me,
	I shall beseech him to befriend himself.
PORTIA	Why, know'st thou any harm's intended towards him? 30
SOOTH.	None that I know will be, much that I fear may chance.
	Good morrow to you. Here the street is narrow:
	The throng that follows Cæsar at the heels,
	Of senators, of prætors, common suitors,
	Will crowd a feeble man almost to death:
	I'll get me to a place more void, and there
	Speak to great Cæsar as he comes along. [*Exit.*
PORTIA	I must go in. [*Aside:*] Ay me, how weak a thing
	The heart of woman is! O Brutus,
	The heavens speed thee in thine enterprise! 40
	Sure, the boy heard me. [*To Lucius:*] Brutus hath a suit
	That Cæsar will not grant. O, I grow faint.[58]
	Run, Lucius, and commend me to my lord;
	Say I am merry. Come to me again,
	And bring me word what he doth say to thee.
	[*Exeunt separately.*

ACT 3, SCENE I.

Initially, the characters speak in the street outside the Capitol's Senate House. Later, they speak within the Senate House, where a statue of Pompey stands.

Enter ARTEMIDORUS, *the* SOOTHSAYER *and* CITIZENS. *Flourish. Enter* CÆSAR, BRUTUS, CASSIUS, CASKA, DECIUS, LIGARIUS, METELLUS, TREBONIUS, CINNA, ANTONY, LEPIDUS, POPILLIUS, PUBLIUS, *and other* SENATORS.

CÆSAR	[*to the Soothsayer:*] The Ides of March are come.
SOOTH.	Ay, Cæsar; but not gone.
ARTEM.	Hail, Cæsar! Read this schedule.
DECIUS	Trebonius doth desire you to o'er-read
	(At your best leisure) this his humble suit.
ARTEM.	O Cæsar, read mine first; for mine's a suit
	That touches Cæsar nearer. Read it, great Cæsar.
CÆSAR	What touches us ourself shall be last served.[59]
ARTEM.	Delay not, Cæsar, read it instantly.
CÆSAR	What, is the fellow mad?
PUBLIUS	[*To Artemidorus:*] Sirrah, give place. 10
CASSIUS	What, urge you your petitions in the street?
	Come to the Capitol.

              [*Cæsar enters the Senate House, the rest following.*

POPILLIUS	[*to Cassius:*] I wish your enterprise today may thrive.
CASSIUS	What enterprise, Popillius?
POPILLIUS	Fare you well.

                    [*He approaches Cæsar.*

BRUTUS	[*to Cassius:*] What said Popillius Lena?
CASSIUS	He wished today our enterprise might thrive.
	I fear our purpose is discoverèd.
BRUTUS	Look how he makes to Cæsar: mark him.
CASSIUS	Caska,
	Be sudden, for we fear prevention.
	– Brutus, what shall be done? If this be known, 20
	Cassius or Cæsar never shall turn back,
	For I will slay myself.
BRUTUS	Cassius, be constant.

Popillius Lena speaks not of our purposes;
For, look, he smiles, and Cæsar doth not change.[60]

CASSIUS   Trebonius knows his time; for, look you, Brutus,
He draws Mark Antony out of the way.
                              [*Exeunt Antony and Trebonius.*

DECIUS   Where is Metellus Cimber? Let him go
And presently prefer his suit to Cæsar.

BRUTUS   He is addressed: press near and second him.

CINNA   Caska, you are the first that rears your hand.   30
                    [*The conspirators and others take their places.*

CÆSAR   Are we all ready? What is now amiss
That Cæsar and his Senate must redress?

METELLUS   [*approaching Cæsar with others, bowing deeply:*]
Most high, most mighty, and most puissant Cæsar,
Metellus Cimber throws before thy seat
An humble heart –

CÆSAR   I must prevent thee, Cimber.
These couchings and these lowly courtesies
Might fire the blood of ordinary men,
And turn pre-ordinance and first decree
Into the law of children.[61] Be not fond
To think that Cæsar bears such rebel blood   40
That will be thawed from the true quality
With that which melteth fools: I mean, sweet words,
Low-crookèd curtsies and base spaniel fawning.
Thy brother by decree is banishèd:
If thou dost bend and pray and fawn for him,
I spurn thee like a cur out of my way.[62]
Know, Cæsar doth not wrong, nor without cause
Will he be satisfied.[63]

METELLUS   Is there no voice more worthy than my own
To sound more sweetly in great Cæsar's ear   50
For the repealing of my banished brother?

BRUTUS   I kiss thy hand, but not in flattery, Cæsar;
Desiring thee that Publius Cimber may
Have an immediate freedom of repeal.

CÆSAR   What, Brutus?

CASSIUS   [*prostrating himself:*] Pardon, Cæsar; Cæsar, pardon:
As low as to thy foot doth Cassius fall,

To beg enfranchisement for Publius Cimber.

CÆSAR   I could be well moved, if I were as you;
If I could pray to move, prayers would move me.
But I am constant as the Northern Star,   60
Of whose true fixed and resting quality
There is no fellow in the firmament.
The skies are painted with unnumbered sparks;
They are all fire, and every one doth shine;
But there's but one in all doth hold his place.
So in the world: 'tis furnished well with men,
And men are flesh and blood, and apprehensive;
Yet, in the number, I do know but one
That unassailable holds on his rank,
Unshaked of motion; and, that I am he,   70
Let me a little show it, even in this:
That I was constant Cimber should be banished,
And constant do remain to keep him so.[64]

CINNA   [*kneels.*] O Cæsar –

CÆSAR   Hence! Wilt thou lift up Olympus?[65]

DECIUS   [*kneels.*] Great Cæsar –

CÆSAR   Doth not Brutus bootless kneel?

CASKA   Speak, hands, for me!

The conspirators stab Cæsar: Caska first, Brutus last. Cæsar, near
Pompey's statue,[66] covers his own face as Brutus strikes.

CÆSAR   *Et tu, Brute?*[67] – Then fall, Cæsar!   [*He falls and dies.*

CINNA   Liberty! Freedom! Tyranny is dead!
Run hence, proclaim, cry it about the streets.

CASSIUS   Some to the common pulpits, and cry out   80
'Liberty, freedom and enfranchisement!'
         [*Exeunt Lepidus, Popillius, Artemidorus, Soothsayer and*
                                      others.

BRUTUS   People and senators, be not affrighted;
Fly not; stand still! Ambition's debt is paid.

CASKA   Go to the pulpit, Brutus.

DECIUS   And Cassius too.

BRUTUS   Where's Publius?

CINNA   Here, quite confounded with this mutiny.

METELLUS   Stand fast together, lest some friend of Cæsar's
Should chance –

BRUTUS   Talk not of standing. – Publius, good cheer;
           There is no harm intended to your person,   90
           Nor to no Roman else: so tell them, Publius.

CASSIUS   And leave us, Publius, lest that the people,
           Rushing on us, should do your age some mischief.

BRUTUS   Do so, and let no man abide this deed
           But we the doers.   [*Exit Publius.*

                    Enter TREBONIUS.

CASSIUS   Where is Antony?

TREBON.   Fled to his house amazed.
           Men, wives and children stare, cry out and run
           As it were Doomsday.

BRUTUS   Fates, we will know your pleasures.
           That we shall die, we know; 'tis but the time,
           And drawing days out, that men stand upon.   100

CASKA   Why, he that cuts off twenty years of life
           Cuts off so many years of fearing death.

BRUTUS   Grant that, and then is death a benefit:
           So are we Cæsar's friends, that have abridged
           His time of fearing death. Stoop, Romans, stoop,
           And let us bathe our hands in Cæsar's blood
           Up to the elbows, and besmear our swords;
           Then walk we forth, even to the market-place,
           And waving our red weapons o'er our heads,
           Let's all cry 'Peace, freedom and liberty!'[68]   110

CASSIUS   Stoop then, and wash. [*They smear blood.*] How many
                                        ages hence
           Shall this our lofty scene be acted over,
           In states unborn and accents yet unknown?[69]

BRUTUS   How many times shall Cæsar bleed in sport,
           That now on Pompey's basis lies along,
           No worthier than the dust?

CASSIUS   So oft as that shall be,
           So often shall the knot of us be called
           'The men that gave their country liberty'.

DECIUS   What, shall we forth?

CASSIUS   Ay, every man away.
           Brutus shall lead, and we will grace his heels   120
           With the most boldest and best hearts of Rome.

Enter Antony's SERVANT.

BRUTUS   Soft: who comes here? A friend of Antony's.
SERVANT   [*kneels.*] Thus, Brutus, did my master bid me kneel;
            [*He falls.*]Thus did Mark Antony bid me fall down;
            And, being prostrate, thus he bade me say:
            'Brutus is noble, wise, valiant and honest;
            Cæsar was mighty, bold, royal and loving.
            Say, I love Brutus and I honour him;
            Say, I feared Cæsar, honoured him and loved him.
            If Brutus will vouchsafe that Antony   130
            May safely come to him and be resolved
            How Cæsar hath deserved to lie in death,
            Mark Antony shall not love Cæsar dead
            So well as Brutus living, but will follow
            The fortunes and affairs of noble Brutus
            Thoróugh the hazards of this untrod state[70]
            With all true faith.' So says my master Antony.
BRUTUS   Thy master is a wise and valiant Roman;
            I never thought him worse.
            Tell him, so please him come unto this place,   140
            He shall be satisfied, and, by my honour,
            Depart untouched.
SERVANT   I'll fetch him presently.   [*Exit.*
BRUTUS   I know that we shall have him well to friend.
CASSIUS   I wish we may; but yet have I a mind
            That fears him much, and my misgiving still
            Falls shrewdly to the purpose.[71]

Enter ANTONY.

BRUTUS   But here comes Antony. – Welcome, Mark Antony.
                        [*Antony approaches the corpse.*
ANTONY   O mighty Cæsar! Dost thou lie so low?
            Are all thy conquests, glories, triumphs, spoils,
            Shrunk to this little measure? Fare thee well.   150
            – I know not, gentlemen, what you intend,
            Who else must be let blood, who else is rank:
            If I myself, there is no hour so fit
            As Cæsar's death's hour, nor no instrument
            Of half that worth as those your swords, made rich

With the most noble blood of all this world.
I do beseech ye, if you bear me hard,
Now, whilst your purpled hands do reek and smoke,
Fulfil your pleasure. Live a thousand years,
I shall not find myself so apt to die: 160
No place will please me so, no mean of death,
As here by Cæsar, and by you cut off,
The choice and master spirits of this age.

BRUTUS   O Antony, beg not your death of us.
Though now we must appear bloody and cruel,
As, by our hands and this our present act,
You see we do; yet see you but our hands
And this the bleeding business they have done.
Our hearts you see not: they are pitiful;
And pity to the general wrong of Rome   170
(As fire drives out fire, so pity pity)[72]
Hath done this deed on Cæsar. For your part,
To you our swords have leaden points, Mark Antony:
Our arms in strength of malice, and our hearts
Of brothers' temper,[73] do receive you in
With all kind love, good thoughts and reverence.

CASSIUS   Your voice shall be as strong as any man's,
In the disposing of new dignities.

BRUTUS   Only be patient till we have appeased
The multitude, beside themselves with fear,   180
And then we will deliver you the cause
Why I, that did love Cæsar when I struck him,
Have thus proceeded.

ANTONY   I doubt not of your wisdom.
Let each man render me his bloody hand.
First, Marcus Brutus, will I shake with you; —
Next, Caius Cassius, do I take your hand; —
Now, Decius Brutus, yours; — now yours, Metellus; —
Yours, Cinna; — and, my valiant Caska, yours; —
Though last, not least in love, yours, good Trebonius.
Gentlemen all: alas, what shall I say?   190
My credit now stands on such slippery ground
That one of two bad ways you must conceit me:
Either a coward or a flatterer.

– That I did love thee, Cæsar, O, 'tis true.
If then thy spirit look upon us now,
Shall it not grieve thee dearer than thy death,
To see thy Antony making his peace,
Shaking the bloody fingers of thy foes?
Most noble,[74] in the presence of thy corse!
Had I as many eyes thou hast wounds,   200
Weeping as fast as they stream forth thy blood,
It would become me better than to close
In terms of friendship with thine enemies.
Pardon me, Julius! Here wast thou bayed, brave hart;
Here didst thou fall, and here thy hunters stand,
Signed in thy spoil and crimsoned in thy Lethe.[75]
O world, thou wast the forest to this hart;
And this, indeed, O world, the heart of thee.
How like a deer strucken by many princes
Dost thou here lie!   210

CASSIUS   Mark Antony –
ANTONY   Pardon me, Caius Cassius:
The enemies of Cæsar shall say this;
Then, in a friend, it is cold modesty.

CASSIUS   I blame you not for praising Cæsar so,
But what compáct mean you to have with us?
Will you be pricked in number of our friends,
Or shall we on, and not depend on you?

ANTONY   Therefore I took your hands, but was indeed
Swayed from the point by looking down on Cæsar.
Friends am I with you all, and love you all,   220
Upon this hope: that you shall give me reasons
Why, and wherein, Cæsar was dangerous.

BRUTUS   Or else were this a savage spectacle.
Our reasons are so full of good regard
That were you, Antony, the son of Cæsar,
You should be satisfied.

ANTONY   That's all I seek,
And am moreover suitor that I may
Produce his body to the market-place,
And in the pulpit (as becomes a friend)
Speak in the order of his funeral.   230

BRUTUS   You shall, Mark Antony.
CASSIUS   [*aside to Brutus:*]   Brutus, a word with you.
            You know not what you do. Do not consent
            That Antony speak in his funeral.
            Know you how much the people may be moved
            By that which he will utter?
BRUTUS   [*aside to Cassius:*]   By your pardon:
            I will myself into the pulpit first,
            And show the reason of our Cæsar's death.
            What Antony shall speak, I will protest
            He speaks by leave and by permission,
            And that we are contented Cæsar shall   240
            Have all true rites and lawful cer'monies.
            It shall advantage more than do us wrong.
CASSIUS   [*aside to him:*] I know not what may fall; I like it not.
BRUTUS   Mark Antony, here, take you Cæsar's body.
            You shall not in your funeral speech blame us,
            But speak all good you can devise of Cæsar;
            And say you do't by our permission;
            Else shall you not have any hand at all
            About his funeral. And you shall speak
            In the same pulpit whereto I am going,   250
            After my speech is ended.
ANTONY   Be it so;
            I do desire no more.
BRUTUS   Prepare the body then, and follow us.
                       [*Exeunt all except Antony, who turns to the corpse.*
ANTONY   O, pardon me, thou bleeding piece of earth,
            That I am meek and gentle with these butchers!
            Thou art the ruins of the noblest man
            That ever livèd in the tide of times.
            Woe to the hands[76] that shed this costly blood!
            Over thy wounds now do I prophesy
            (Which like dumb mouths do ope their ruby lips   260
            To beg the voice and utterance of my tongue),
            A curse shall light upon the limbs of men:
            Domestic fury and fierce civil strife
            Shall cumber all the parts of Italy;
            Blood and destruction shall be so in use,

And dreadful objects so familiar,
That mothers shall but smile when they behold
Their infants quartered with the hands of war,
All pity choked with custom of fell deeds;
And Cæsar's spirit, ranging for revenge,   270
With Ate[77] by his side come hot from Hell,
Shall in these confines with a monarch's voice
Cry 'Havoc!' and let slip the dogs of war,[78]
That this foul deed shall smell above the earth
With carrion men, groaning for burial.

Enter Octavius' SERVANT.

            – You serve Octavius Cæsar, do you not?
SERVANT   I do, Mark Antony.
ANTONY   Cæsar did write for him to come to Rome.[79]
SERVANT   He did receive his letters, and is coming,
And bid me say to you by word of mouth –   280
[*He sees the corpse:*] O Cæsar!
ANTONY   Thy heart is big; get thee apart and weep.
Passion, I see, is catching, for mine eyes,[80]
Seeing those beads of sorrow stand in thine,
Began to water. Is thy master coming?
SERVANT   He lies tonight within seven leagues of Rome.
ANTONY   Post back with speed, and tell him what hath chanced.
Here is a mourning Rome, a dangerous Rome,
No Rome of safety for Octavius yet.
Hie hence, and tell him so. Yet stay a while;   290
Thou shalt not back till I have borne this corse
Into the market-place: there shall I try,
In my oration, how the people take
The cruel issue of these bloody men;
According to the which, thou shalt discourse
To young Octavius of the state of things.
Lend me your hand.
                      [*Exeunt, carrying the corpse.*

SCENE 2.

The Forum, with a pulpit.

Enter BRUTUS, CASSIUS, *and a crowd of* PLEBEIANS.

PLEBEIANS We will be satisfied; let us be satisfied.

BRUTUS   Then follow me, and give me audience, friends.
            – Cassius, go you into the other street,
          And part the numbers.
            – Those that will hear me speak, let 'em stay here;
          Those that will follow Cassius, go with him;
          And public reasons shall be renderèd
          Of Cæsar's death.

PLEB. 1   I will hear Brutus speak.

PLEB. 2   I will hear Cassius, and compare their reasons,
          When severally we hear them renderèd.   10

                    [*Exit Cassius with some of the plebeians.*
                         Brutus goes up into the pulpit.

PLEB. 3   The noble Brutus is ascended: silence!

BRUTUS   Be patient till the last.[81]

          Romans, countrymen, and lovers! Hear me for my
          cause, and be silent, that you may hear. Believe me for
          mine honour, and have respect to mine honour, that
          you may believe. Censure me in your wisdom, and
          awake your senses, that you may the better judge. If
          there be any in this assembly, any dear friend of Cæsar's,
          to him I say that Brutus' love to Cæsar was no less than
          his. If, then, that friend demand why Brutus rose against 20
          Cæsar, this is my answer: not that I loved Cæsar less, but
          that I loved Rome more. Had you rather Cæsar were
          living, and die all slaves, than that Cæsar were dead, to
          live all free men? As Cæsar loved me, I weep for him; as
          he was fortunate, I rejoice at it; as he was valiant, I
          honour him; but, as he was ambitious, I slew him.
          There is tears, for his love; joy, for his fortune; honour,
          for his valour; and death, for his ambition. Who is here
          so base, that would be a bondman? If any, speak; for
          him have I offended. Who is here so rude, that would   30

not be a Roman? If any, speak; for him have I offended. Who is here so vile, that will not love his country? If any, speak; for him have I offended. I pause for a reply.

CROWD None, Brutus, none.

BRUTUS Then none have I offended. I have done no more to Cæsar than you shall do to Brutus.[82] The question of his death is enrolled in the Capitol: his glory not extenuated, wherein he was worthy, nor his offences enforced, for which he suffered death.

Enter ANTONY, *with* BEARERS *carrying Cæsar's mantle-covered corpse in an open coffin.*

Here comes his body, mourned by Mark Antony, who, 40 though he had no hand in his death, shall receive the benefit of his dying, a place in the commonwealth; as which of you shall not? With this I depart: that, as I slew my best lover for the good of Rome, I have the same dagger for myself, when it shall please my country to need my death.

CROWD Live, Brutus! Live, live!

PLEB. I Bring him with triumph home unto his house.

PLEB. 4 Give him a statue with his ancestors.[83]

PLEB. 3 Let him be Cæsar!

PLEB. 5 Cæsar's better parts 50
Shall be crowned in Brutus.

PLEB. I We'll bring him to his house with shouts and clamours.

BRUTUS My countrymen —

PLEB. 4 Peace, silence! Brutus speaks.

PLEB. I Peace, ho!

BRUTUS Good countrymen, let me depart alone,
And (for my sake) stay here with Antony.
Do grace to Cæsar's corpse, and grace his speech
Tending to Cæsar's glories, which Mark Antony
(By our permission) is allowed to make.
I do entreat you, not a man depart, 60
Save I alone, till Antony have spoke. [*Exit.*

PLEB. I Stay, ho! And let us hear Mark Antony.

PLEB. 3 Let him go up into the public chair;
We'll hear him. — Noble Antony, go up.

ANTONY For Brutus' sake, I am beholding to you.

[*He goes up into the pulpit.*

PLEB. 5   What does he say of Brutus?

PLEB. 3   He says, for Brutus' sake,
He finds himself beholding to us all.

PLEB. 5   'Twere best he speak no harm of Brutus here.

PLEB. I   This Cæsar was a tyrant.

PLEB. 3   Nay, that's certain:
We are blest that Rome is rid of him.   70

PLEB. 4   Peace! Let us hear what Antony can say.

ANTONY   You gentle Romans –

CROWD   Peace, ho! Let us hear him.

ANTONY   Friends, Romans, countrymen: lend me your ears!
I come to bury Cæsar, not to praise him.
The evil that men do lives after them,
The good is oft interrèd with their bones:
So let it be with Cæsar.[84] The noble Brutus
Hath told you Cæsar was ambitious:[85]
If it were so, it was a grievous fault,
And grievously hath Cæsar answered it.   80
Here, under leave of Brutus and the rest
(For Brutus is an honourable man;
So are they all; all honourable men),
Come I to speak in Cæsar's funeral.
He was my friend, faithful and just to me;
But Brutus says, he was ambitious;
And Brutus is an honourable man.
He hath brought many captives home to Rome,
Whose ransoms did the general coffers fill:
Did this in Cæsar seem ambitious?   90
When that the poor have cried, Cæsar hath wept:
Ambition should be made of sterner stuff;
Yet Brutus says, he was ambitious;
And Brutus is an honourable man.
You all did see that on the Lupercal
I thrice presented him a kingly crown,
Which he did thrice refuse. Was this ambition?
Yet Brutus says, he was ambitious;
And, sure, he is an honourable man.
I speak not to disprove what Brutus spoke,   100

But here I am to speak what I do know.
You all did love him once, not without cause:
What cause withholds you, then, to mourn for him?
O judgement! Thou art fled to brutish beasts,[86]
And men have lost their reason. Bear with me;
My heart is in the coffin there with Cæsar,
And I must pause till it come back to me.

PLEB. 1 Methinks there is much reason in his sayings.

PLEB. 4 If thou consider rightly of the matter,
Cæsar has had great wrong.

PLEB. 3   Has he, masters?   110
I fear there will a worse come in his place.

PLEB. 5 Marked ye his words? He would not take the crown;
Therefore 'tis certain he was not ambitious.

PLEB. 1 If it be found so, some will dear abide it.

PLEB. 4 Poor soul! His eyes are red as fire with weeping.

PLEB. 3 There's not a nobler man in Rome than Antony.

PLEB. 4 Now mark him: he begins again to speak.

ANTONY But yesterday, the word of Cæsar might
Have stood against the world. Now lies he there,
And none so poor to do him reverence.   120
O masters! If I were disposed to stir
Your hearts and minds to mutiny and rage,
I should do Brutus wrong and Cassius wrong,
Who (you all know) are honourable men.
I will not do them wrong; I rather choose
To wrong the dead, to wrong myself and you,
Than I will wrong such honourable men.
But here's a parchment with the seal of Cæsar.
I found it in his closet: 'tis his will.
Let but the commons hear this testament –   130
Which (pardon me) I do not mean to read –
And they would go and kiss dead Cæsar's wounds,
And dip their napkins in his sacred blood,
Yea, beg a hair of him for memory,
And, dying, mention it within their wills,
Bequeathing it as a rich legacy
Unto their issue.

PLEB. 5 We'll hear the will: read it, Mark Antony.

CROWD   The will, the will; we will hear Cæsar's will!

ANTONY   Have patience, gentle friends, I must not read it.   140
          It is not meet you know how Cæsar loved you.
          You are not wood, you are not stones, but men;
          And, being men, hearing the will of Cæsar,
          It will inflame you, it will make you mad.
          'Tis good you know not that you are his heirs;
          For if you should, O what would come of it?

PLEB. 5   Read the will; we'll hear it, Antony.
          You shall read us the will, Cæsar's will.

ANTONY   Will you be patient? Will you stay awhile?
          I have o'ershot myself to tell you of it: 150
          I fear I wrong the honourable men
          Whose daggers have stabbed Cæsar; I do fear it.

PLEB. 4   They were traitors: 'honourable men'?

CROWD   The will! The testament!

PLEB. 5   They were villains, murderers! The will: read the will!

ANTONY   You will compel me then to read the will.
          Then make a ring about the corpse of Cæsar,
          And let me show you him that made the will.
          Shall I descend? And will you give me leave?

CROWD   Come down.   160

PLEB. 4   Descend.

PLEB. 3   You shall have leave.   [Antony comes down.

PLEB. 5   A ring; stand round.

PLEB. 1   Stand from the hearse, stand from the body.

PLEB. 4   Room for Antony, most noble Antony.

ANTONY   Nay, press not so upon me; stand far off.

CROWD   Stand back: room! Bear back!

ANTONY   If you have tears, prepare to shed them now.
          You all do know this mantle. I remember
          The first time ever Cæsar put it on: 170
          'Twas on a summer's evening, in his tent,
          That day he overcame the Nervii.[87]
          Look, in this place ran Cassius' dagger through;
          See what a rent the envious Caska made;
          Through this the well-belovèd Brutus stabbed,
          And as he plucked his cursèd steel away,
          Mark how the blood of Cæsar followed it,

As rushing out of doors, to be resolved
If Brutus so unkindly knocked, or no:
For Brutus, as you know, was Cæsar's angel.   180
Judge, O you gods, how dearly Cæsar loved him!
This was the most unkindest cut of all;[88]
For when the noble Cæsar saw him stab,
Ingratitude, more strong than traitors' arms,
Quite vanquished him: then burst his mighty heart;
And, in his mantle muffling up his face,
Even at the base of Pompey's statua
(Which all the while ran blood), great Cæsar fell.
O, what a fall was there, my countrymen!
Then I, and you, and all of us fell down,   190
Whilst bloody Treason flourished over us.
O, now you weep, and I perceive you feel
The dint of pity: these are gracious drops.
Kind souls, what, weep you when you but behold
Our Cæsar's vesture wounded? Look you here,
Here is himself, marred, as you see, with traitors.
                    [*He removes the mantle to reveal the corpse.*

PLEB. I	O piteous spectacle!
PLEB. 4	O noble Cæsar!
PLEB. 3	O woeful day!
PLEB. 5	O traitors, villains! 200
PLEB. I	O most bloody sight!
PLEB. 4	We will be revenged.
CROWD	Revenge! About! Seek! Burn! Fire! Kill! Slay!
	Let not a traitor live!
ANTONY	Stay, countrymen.
PLEB. I	Peace there! Hear the noble Antony.
PLEB. 4	We'll hear him, we'll follow him, we'll die with him!
ANTONY	Good friends, sweet friends, let me not stir you up

To such a sudden flood of mutiny:
They that have done this deed are honourable.
What private griefs they have, alas, I know not,   210
That made them do it: they are wise and honourable,
And will, no doubt, with reasons answer you.
I come not, friends, to steal away your hearts:
I am no orator, as Brutus is,

But (as you know me all) a plain blunt man
That love my friend; and that they know full well
That gave me public leave to speak of him:
For I have neither wit,[89] nor words, nor worth,
Action, nor utterance, nor the power of speech,
To stir men's blood. I only speak right on: 220
I tell you that which you yourselves do know,
Show you sweet Cæsar's wounds, poor poor
                                        dumb mouths,
And bid them speak for me; but were I Brutus,
And Brutus Antony, there were an Antony
Would ruffle up your spirits, and put a tongue
In every wound of Cæsar, that should move
The stones of Rome to rise and mutiny.[90]

CROWD   We'll mutiny!
PLEB. 1   We'll burn the house of Brutus.
PLEB. 3   Away, then! Come, seek the conspirators.
ANTONY   Yet hear me, countrymen; yet hear me speak.   230
CROWD   Peace, ho! Hear Antony, most noble Antony!
ANTONY   Why, friends, you go to do you know not what.
           Wherein hath Cæsar thus deserved your loves?
           Alas, you know not; I must tell you then.
           You have forgot the will I told you of.
CROWD   Most true: the will! Let's stay and hear the will!
ANTONY   Here is the will, and under Cæsar's seal.
           To every Roman citizen he gives,
           To every several man, seventy-five drachmas.[91]
PLEB. 4   Most noble Cæsar! We'll revenge his death.   240
PLEB. 3   O royal Cæsar!
ANTONY   Hear me with patience.
CROWD   Peace, ho!
ANTONY   Moreover, he hath left you all his walks,
           His private arbours and new-planted orchards,
           On this side Tiber. He hath left them you,
           And to your heirs for ever; common pleasures,
           To walk abroad and recreate yourselves.
           Here was a Cæsar: when comes such another?
PLEB. 1   Never, never. Come, away, away!
           We'll burn his body in the holy place,   250

            And with the brands fire the traitors' houses.
            Take up the body.

PLEB. 4   Go fetch fire.

PLEB. 3   Pluck down benches.

PLEB. 5   Pluck down forms, windows, anything!

         [*Exeunt plebeians, diversely, and bearers carrying the coffin.*

ANTONY   Now let it work. Mischief, thou art afoot,
            Take thou what course thou wilt.

               Enter Octavius' SERVANT.

                              How now, fellow?

SERVANT   Sir, Octavius is already come to Rome.

ANTONY   Where is he?

SERVANT   He and Lepidus are at Cæsar's house.[92]   260

ANTONY   And thither will I straight to visit him:
            He comes upon a wish. Fortune is merry,
            And in this mood will give us any thing.

SERVANT   I heard him say, Brutus and Cassius
            Are rid like madmen through the gates of Rome.

ANTONY   Belike they had some notice of the people,
            How I had moved them. Bring me to Octavius.

                                 [*Exeunt.*

SCENE 3.

Enter CINNA *the poet, followed by* PLEBEIANS.

CINNA   I dreamt tonight that I did feast with Cæsar,
            And things unluckily charge my fantasy.[93]
            I have no will to wander forth of doors,
            Yet something leads me forth.

                             [*Plebeians accost him.*

PLEB. 1   What is your name?

PLEB. 2   Whither are you going?

PLEB. 3   Where do you dwell?

PLEB. 4   Are you a married man or a bachelor?

PLEB. 2   Answer every man directly.

PLEB. 1   Ay, and briefly.   10

PLEB. 4   Ay, and wisely.

PLEB. 3	Ay, and truly, you were best.
CINNA	What is my name? Whither am I going? Where do I dwell? Am I a married man or a bachelor? Then, to answer every man directly and briefly, wisely and truly: wisely I say, I am a bachelor.
PLEB. 2	That's as much as to say, they are fools that marry: you'll bear me a bang for that, I fear. Proceed directly.
CINNA	Directly, I am going to Cæsar's funeral.
PLEB. 1	As a friend or an enemy?
CINNA	As a friend.
PLEB. 2	That matter is answered directly.
PLEB. 4	For your dwelling, briefly.
CINNA	Briefly, I dwell by the Capitol.
PLEB. 3	Your name, sir, truly.
CINNA	Truly, my name is Cinna.
PLEB. 1	Tear him to pieces: he's a conspirator!
CINNA	I am Cinna the poet, I am Cinna the poet!
PLEB. 4	Tear him for his bad verses, tear him for his bad verses!
CINNA	I am not Cinna the conspirator.
PLEB. 4	It is no matter, his name's Cinna; pluck but his name out of his heart, and turn him going.
PLEB. 3	Tear him, tear him! [*They murder Cinna the poet.*[94]] Come, brands ho, fire-brands! To Brutus', to Cassius': burn all! Some to Decius' house, and some to Caska's; some to Ligarius'! Away, go!

20

30

[*Exeunt plebeians.*

ACT 4, SCENE I.

A room in Antony's house.

Enter ANTONY *(with papers),* OCTAVIUS *and* LEPIDUS.

ANTONY   These many then shall die; their names are pricked.

OCTAVIUS [*to Lepidus:*] Your brother too must die; consent you,
                                                    Lepidus?

LEPIDUS   I do consent –

OCTAVIUS   Prick him down, Antony, –

LEPIDUS   Upon condition Publius shall not live,
          Who is your sister's son, Mark Antony.[95]

ANTONY   He shall not live; look, with a spot I damn him.
          But, Lepidus, go you to Cæsar's house:
          Fetch the will hither, and we shall determine
          How to cut off some charge in legacies.[96]

LEPIDUS   What, shall I find you here?   10

OCTAVIUS Or here or at the Capitol.   [*Exit Lepidus.*

ANTONY   This is a slight unmeritable man,
          Meet to be sent on errands. Is it fit,
          The three-fold world divided, he should stand
          One of the three to share it?[97]

OCTAVIUS   So you thought him,
          And took his voice who should be pricked to die
          In our black sentence and proscription.[98]

ANTONY   Octavius, I have seen more days than you;
          And though we lay these honours on this man
          To ease ourselves of divers sland'rous loads,   20
          He shall but bear them as the ass bears gold,
          To groan and sweat under the business,[99]
          Either led or driven, as we point the way;
          And having brought our treasure where we will,
          Then take we down his load and turn him off,
          Like to the empty ass, to shake his ears
          And graze in commons.

OCTAVIUS   You may do your will;
          But he's a tried and valiant soldier.

ANTONY   So is my horse, Octavius, and for that

I do appoint him store of provender.   30
It is a creature that I teach to fight,
To wind, to stop, to run directly on,
His corporal motion governed by my spirit;
And in some taste is Lepidus but so:
He must be taught, and trained, and bid go forth;
A barren-spirited fellow, one that feeds
On objects, arts, and imitations[100]
Which, out of use and staled by other men,
Begin his fashion. Do not talk of him
But as a property.[101] And now, Octavius,   40
Listen great things. Brutus and Cassius
Are levying powers: we must straight make head.
Therefore let our alliance be combined,
Our best friends made, our means stretched;[102]
And let us presently go sit in council,
How covert matters may be best disclosed,
And open perils surest answerèd.
OCTAVIUS Let us do so: for we are at the stake,
And bayed about with many enemies;[103]
And some that smile have in their hearts, I fear,   50
Millions of mischiefs.

                                              [*Exeunt.*

SCENE 2.

Before Brutus' tent in the camp near Sardis.

Drum sounds. Enter BRUTUS, LUCIUS *and* SOLDIERS *from one direction,
meeting* LUCILLIUS, TITINIUS, PINDARUS
and SOLDIERS *from another direction.*[104]

BRUTUS   Stand, ho!
LUCILLIUS Give the word, ho, and stand!   [*Soldiers halt.*
BRUTUS   What now, Lucillius: is Cassius near?
LUCILLIUS He is at hand, and Pindarus is come
           To do you salutation from his master.
BRUTUS   He greets me well. – Your master, Pindarus,
           In his own change, or by ill officers,[105]
           Hath given me some worthy cause to wish

Things done undone; but if he be at hand,
I shall be satisfied.

PINDARUS   I do not doubt   10
But that my noble master will appear
Such as he is, full of regard and honour.

BRUTUS   He is not doubted. A word, Lucillius:
                            [*Brutus and Lucillius speak privately.*
How he received you, let me be resolved.

LUCILLIUS With courtesy and with respect enough,
But not with such familiar instances,
Nor with such free and friendly conference,
As he hath used of old.

BRUTUS   Thou hast described
A hot friend cooling. Ever note, Lucillius,
When love begins to sicken and decay,   20
It useth an enforcèd cer'mony.
There are no tricks in plain and simple faith;
But hollow men, like horses hot at hand,
Make gallant show and promise of their mettle,
But when they should endure the bloody spur,
They fall their crests and, like deceitful jades,
Sink in the trial. Comes his army on?

LUCILLIUS They mean this night in Sardis to be quartered;
The greater part, the horse in general,
Are come with Cassius.   [*Drums heard.*

BRUTUS   Hark, he is arrived.   30
    – March gently on to meet him.   [*Soldiers march.*

                Enter CASSIUS *and his* SOLDIERS.

CASSIUS   Stand, ho!   [*His soldiers halt.*
BRUTUS   Stand, ho! Speak the word along.
SOLDIER 1 Stand!
SOLDIER 2 Stand!
SOLDIER 3 Stand!   [*Brutus' soldiers halt.*
CASSIUS   Most noble brother, you have done me wrong.
BRUTUS   Judge me, you gods; wrong I mine enemies?
And, if not so, how should I wrong a brother?
CASSIUS   Brutus, this sober form of yours hides wrongs,   40
And when you do them –
BRUTUS   Cassius, be content;

Speak your griefs softly. I do know you well.
Before the eyes of both our armies here
(Which should perceive nothing but love from us),
Let us not wrangle. Bid them move away;
Then in my tent, Cassius, enlarge your griefs,
And I will give you audience.

CASSIUS   Pindarus,
Bid our commanders lead their charges off
A little from this ground.

BRUTUS   Lucillius, do you the like, and let no man   50
Come to our tent till we have done our conference.
Let Lucius and Titinius guard our door.

> [*Exeunt all except Lucius, Titinius, Brutus and Cassius.*
> *While Lucius and Titinius guard the entrance, Brutus and*
> *Cassius enter the tent.*[106]

CASSIUS   That you have wronged me doth appear in this:
You have condemned and noted Lucius Pella
For taking bribes here of the Sardians;
Wherein my letters, praying on his side
Because I knew the man, was slighted off.

BRUTUS   You wronged yourself to write in such a case.

CASSIUS   In such a time as this, it is not meet
That every nice offence should bear his comment.[107]   60

BRUTUS   Let me tell you, Cassius, you yourself
Are much condemned to have an itching palm,
To sell and mart your offices for gold
To undeservers.

CASSIUS   I, 'an itching palm'?
You know that you are Brutus that speaks this,
Or, by the gods, this speech were else your last.

BRUTUS   The name of Cassius honours this corruption,
And chástisement doth therefore hide his head.

CASSIUS   'Chástisement'?

BRUTUS   Remember March, the Ides of March remember: 70
Did not great Julius bleed for justice' sake?
What villain touched his body, that did stab,
And not for justice? What, shall one of us,
That struck the foremost man of all this world
But for supporting robbers,[108] shall we now

            Contaminate our fingers with base bribes,
            And sell the mighty space of our large honours
            For so much trash as may be graspèd thus?
            I had rather be a dog, and bay the moon,
            Than such a Roman.

CASSIUS   Brutus, bait not me;[109]   80
            I'll not endure it; you forget yourself,
            To hedge me in. I am a soldier, I,
            Older in practice, abler than yourself
            To make conditions.

BRUTUS   Go to; you are not, Cassius.
CASSIUS   I am.
BRUTUS   I say you are not.
CASSIUS   Urge me no more; I shall forget myself.
            Have mind upon your health: tempt me no farther.
BRUTUS   Away, slight man!
CASSIUS   Is't possible?
BRUTUS   Hear me, for I will speak.   90
            Must I give way and room to your rash choler?
            Shall I be frighted when a madman stares?
CASSIUS   O ye gods, ye gods! Must I endure all this?
BRUTUS   'All this?' Ay, more: fret till your proud heart break.
            Go show your slaves how choleric you are,
            And make your bondmen tremble. Must I budge?
            Must I observe you? Must I stand and crouch
            Under your testy humour? By the gods,
            You shall digest the venom of your spleen,
            Though it do split you; for, from this day forth,   100
            I'll use you for my mirth, yea, for my laughter,
            When you are waspish.
CASSIUS   Is it come to this?
BRUTUS   You say you are a better soldier:
            Let it appear so; make your vaunting true,
            And it shall please me well. For mine own part,
            I shall be glad to learn of noble men.
CASSIUS   You wrong me every way; you wrong me, Brutus.
            I said, an elder soldier, not a better.
            Did I say 'better'?
BRUTUS   If you did, I care not.

CASSIUS	When Cæsar lived, he durst not thus have moved me. 110
BRUTUS	Peace, peace; you durst not so have tempted him.
CASSIUS	I durst not?
BRUTUS	No.
CASSIUS	What, durst not tempt him?
BRUTUS	For your life you durst not.
CASSIUS	Do not presume too much upon my love;
	I may do that I shall be sorry for.
BRUTUS	You have done that you should be sorry for.
	There is no terror, Cassius, in your threats,
	For I am armed so strong in honesty
	That they pass by me as the idle wind 120
	Which I respect not. I did send to you
	For certain sums of gold, which you denied me;
	For I can raise no money by vile means:
	By heaven, I had rather coin my heart,
	And drop my blood for drachmas, than to wring
	From the hard hands of peasants their vile trash
	By any indirection. I did send
	To you for gold to pay my legions,
	Which you denied me: was that done like Cassius?
	Should I have answered Caius Cassius so? 130
	When Marcus Brutus grows so covetous
	To lock such rascal counters from his friends,
	Be ready, gods, with all your thunderbolts:
	Dash him to pieces!
CASSIUS	I denied you not.[110]
BRUTUS	You did.
CASSIUS	I did not. He was but a fool
	That brought my answer back. Brutus hath rived
	my heart:
	A friend should bear his friend's infirmities,
	But Brutus makes mine greater than they are.
BRUTUS	I do not, till you practise them on me.
CASSIUS	You love me not.
BRUTUS	I do not like your faults. 140
CASSIUS	A friendly eye could never see such faults.
BRUTUS	A flatterer's would not, though they do appear

As huge as high Olympus.

CASSIUS　　Come, Antony, and young Octavius, come,
Revenge yourselves alone on Cassius,
For Cassius is aweary of the world:
Hated by one he loves, braved by his brother,
Checked like a bondman; all his faults observed,
Set in a note-book, learned and conned by rote,
To cast into my teeth. O, I could weep　　　　　　　150
My spirit from mine eyes! There is my dagger,
And here my naked breast; within, a heart
Dearer than Pluto's mine,[111] richer than gold:
If that thou be'st a Roman, take it forth.
I, that denied thee gold, will give my heart:
Strike, as thou didst at Cæsar; for I know,
When thou didst hate him worst, thou lovedst
　　　　　　　　　　　　　　　　　　him better
Than ever thou lovedst Cassius.

BRUTUS　　　　　　　　　　　　Sheathe your dagger.
Be angry when you will, it shall have scope;
Do what you will, dishonour shall be humour.[112]　　160
O Cassius, you are yokèd with a lamb,
That carries anger as the flint bears fire,
Who, much enforcèd, shows a hasty spark
And straight is cold again.

CASSIUS　　　　　　　　　　　Hath Cassius lived
To be but 'mirth' and 'laughter' to his Brutus,
When grief and blood ill-tempered vexeth him?

BRUTUS　　When I spoke that, I was ill-tempered too.

CASSIUS　　Do you confess so much? Give me your hand.

BRUTUS　　And my heart too.　　　　　　　　[They embrace.

CASSIUS　　　　　　　O Brutus!

BRUTUS　　　　　　　　　　What's the matter?

CASSIUS　　Have not you love enough to bear with me,　　170
When that rash humour which my mother gave me
Makes me forgetful?

BRUTUS　　　　　　　　Yes, Cassius, and from henceforth,
When you are over-earnest with your Brutus,
He'll think your mother chides, and leave you so.

Enter a POET, *struggling with Lucillius. Lucius and Titinius*
help to restrain him.[113]

POET	Let me go in to see the generals;
	There is some grudge between 'em; 'tis not meet
	They be alone.
LUCILLIUS	You shall not come to them.
POET	Nothing but death shall stay me.
CASSIUS	How now? What's the matter?
POET	For shame, you generals! What do you mean? 180
	Love and be friends, as two such men should be;
	For I have seen more years, I'm sure, than ye.
CASSIUS	Ha, ha! How vildely doth this cynic rhyme![114]
BRUTUS	[*to poet:*] Get you hence, sirrah; saucy fellow, hence!
CASSIUS	Bear with him, Brutus; 'tis his fashion.
BRUTUS	I'll know his humour when he knows his time:
	What should the wars do with these jigging fools?[115]
	[*To poet:*] Companion, hence!
CASSIUS	Away, away, be gone!
	[*Exit poet.*
BRUTUS	Lucillius and Titinius, bid the commanders
	Prepare to lodge their companies tonight. 190
CASSIUS	And come yourselves, and bring Messala with you
	Immediately to us. [*Exeunt Lucillius and Titinius.*
BRUTUS	Lucius, a bowl of wine.
	[*Exit Lucius.*
CASSIUS	I did not think you could have been so angry.
BRUTUS	O Cassius, I am sick of many griefs.
CASSIUS	Of your philosophy you make no use,
	If you give place to accidental evils.[116]
BRUTUS	No man bears sorrow better. Portia is dead.[117]
CASSIUS	Ha? Portia?
BRUTUS	She is dead.
CASSIUS	How scaped I killing, when I crossed you so? 200
	O insupportable and touching loss!
	Upon what sickness?
BRUTUS	Impatient of my absence,
	And grief that young Octavius with Mark Antony
	Have made themselves so strong; for with her death
	That tidings came. With this she fell distract,

And (her attendants absent) swallowed fire.

CASSIUS And died so?

BRUTUS   Even so.

CASSIUS   O ye immortal gods!

Enter LUCIUS, *bearing wine and tapers.*

BRUTUS Speak no more of her. – Give me a bowl of wine. –
In this I bury all unkindness, Cassius.   [*He drinks.*

CASSIUS My heart is thirsty for that noble pledge.   210
Fill, Lucius, till the wine o'erswell the cup:
I cannot drink too much of Brutus' love.

                              [*He drinks. Exit Lucius.*

Enter TITINIUS *and* MESSALA.

BRUTUS Come in, Titinius; welcome, good Messala.
Now sit we close about this taper here,
And call in question our necessities.

CASSIUS Portia, art thou gone?

BRUTUS   No more, I pray you.
– Messala, I have here received letters[118]
That young Octavius and Mark Antony
Come down upon us with a mighty power,
Bending their expedition toward Philippi.   220

MESSALA Myself have letters of the selfsame tenor.

BRUTUS With what addition?

MESSALA That by proscription and bills of outlawry,
Octavius, Antony and Lepidus
Have put to death an hundred senators.

BRUTUS Therein our letters do not well agree:
Mine speak of seventy senators that died
By their proscriptions, Cicero being one.

CASSIUS Cicero one?

MESSALA   Cicero is dead,
And by that order of proscription.   230
– Had you your letters from your wife, my lord?

BRUTUS No, Messala.

MESSALA Nor nothing in your letters writ of her?

BRUTUS Nothing, Messala.

MESSALA   That, methinks, is strange.

BRUTUS Why ask you? Hear you aught of her in yours?

MESSALA	No, my lord.
BRUTUS	Now, as you are a Roman, tell me true.
MESSALA	Then, like a Roman, bear the truth I tell:
	For certain she is dead, and by strange manner.
BRUTUS	Why, farewell, Portia. – We must die, Messala: 240
	With meditating that she must die once,
	I have the patience to endure it now.
MESSALA	Even so great men great losses should endure.
CASSIUS	I have as much of this in art as you,
	But yet my nature could not bear it so.
BRUTUS	Well, to our work alive. What do you think
	Of marching to Philippi presently?
CASSIUS	I do not think it good.
BRUTUS	Your reason?
CASSIUS	This it is:
	'Tis better that the enemy seek us:
	So shall he waste his means, weary his soldiers, 250
	Doing himself offence; whilst we, lying still,
	Are full of rest, defence and nimbleness.
BRUTUS	Good reasons must of force give place to better.
	The people 'twixt Philippi and this ground
	Do stand but in a forced affection,
	For they have grudged us contribution.[119]
	The enemy, marching along by them,
	By them shall make a fuller number up,
	Come on refreshed, new added, and encouraged;
	From which advantage shall we cut him off 260
	If at Philippi we do face him there,
	These people at our back.
CASSIUS	Hear me, good brother.
BRUTUS	Under your pardon. You must note beside
	That we have tried the utmost of our friends;
	Our legions are brim-full, our cause is ripe.
	The enemy increaseth every day;
	We, at the height, are ready to decline.
	There is a tide in the affairs of men
	Which, taken at the flood, leads on to fortune;
	Omitted, all the voyage of their life 270
	Is bound in shallows and in miseries.

On such a full sea are we now afloat,
And we must take the current when it serves,
Or lose our ventures.

CASSIUS   Then, with your will, go on;
We'll along ourselves, and meet them at Philippi.[120]

BRUTUS   The deep of night is crept upon our talk;
And nature must obey necessity,
Which we will niggard with a little rest.
There is no more to say.

CASSIUS   No more; good night.
Early tomorrow will we rise and hence.   280

BRUTUS   Lucius!

Enter LUCIUS.

My gown.   [*Exit Lucius.*
Farewell, good Messala; –
Good night, Titinius, – noble, noble Cassius,
Good night, and good repose.

CASSIUS   O my dear brother,
This was an ill beginning of the night:
Never come such division 'tween our souls!
Let it not, Brutus.

Enter LUCIUS *with the gown.*

BRUTUS   Everything is well.

CASSIUS   Good night, my lord.

BRUTUS   Good night, good brother.

TITINIUS, MESSALA   Good night, Lord Brutus.

BRUTUS   Farewell, every one.
[*Exeunt Cassius, Titinius and Messala.*
Give me the gown. Where is thy instrument?

LUCIUS   Here in the tent.   [*Brutus dons the gown.*

BRUTUS   What? Thou speak'st drowsily.   290
Poor knave, I blame thee not; thou art o'erwatched.
Call Claudio and some other of my men;
I'll have them sleep on cushions in my tent.

LUCIUS   [*calling:*] Varrus and Claudio!

Enter VARRUS *and* CLAUDIO.

VARRUS   Calls my lord?

BRUTUS   I pray you, sirs, lie in my tent and sleep;

It may be I shall raise you by and by
On business to my brother Cassius.

VARRUS   So please you, we will stand and watch your pleasure.

BRUTUS   I will not have it so. Lie down, good sirs;   300
It may be I shall otherwise bethink me.

[*Varrus and Claudio lie down.*

– Look, Lucius, here's the book I sought for so;
I put it in the pocket of my gown.

LUCIUS   I was sure your lordship did not give it me.

BRUTUS   Bear with me, good boy; I am much forgetful.
Canst thou hold up thy heavy eyes awhile,
And touch thy instrument a strain or two?

LUCIUS   Ay, my lord, an't please you.

BRUTUS   It does, my boy.
I trouble thee too much, but thou art willing.

LUCIUS   It is my duty, sir.   310

BRUTUS   I should not urge thy duty past thy might:
I know young bloods look for a time of rest.

LUCIUS   I have slept, my lord, already.

BRUTUS   It was well done, and thou shalt sleep again:
I will not hold thee long. If I do live,
I will be good to thee.   [*Lucius plays, sings, and sleeps.*
This is a sleepy tune. – O murd'rous slumber,
Layest thou thy leaden mace upon my boy
That plays thee music? – Gentle knave, good night.
I will not do thee so much wrong to wake thee.   320
If thou dost nod, thou break'st thy instrument:
I'll take it from thee; and, good boy, good night.

[*After removing the instrumnet, he opens the book.*

Lee me see, let me see; is not the leaf turned down
Where I left reading? Here it is, I think.

Enter CÆSAR'S GHOST.

How ill this taper burns. – Ha! Who comes here? –
I think it is the weakness of mine eyes
That shapes this monstrous apparition.
It comes upon me. – Art thou any thing?
Art thou some god, some angel, or some devil,
That mak'st my blood cold, and my hair to stare?   330
Speak to me what thou art.

GHOST	Thy evil spirit, Brutus![121]
BRUTUS	Why com'st thou?
GHOST	To tell thee thou shalt see me at Philippi.
BRUTUS	Well; then I shall see thee again?
GHOST	Ay, at Philippi.
BRUTUS	Why, I will see thee at Philippi then.

[*Exit Ghost.*

Now I have taken heart, thou vanishest.
Ill spirit, I would hold more talk with thee.
– Boy, Lucius! Varrus! Claudio! Sirs, awake!
Claudio!

LUCIUS	The strings, my lord, are false.	340
BRUTUS	He thinks he still is at his instrument.	

– Lucius, awake!

LUCIUS	My lord?
BRUTUS	Didst thou dream, Lucius, that thou so criedst out?
LUCIUS	My lord, I do not know that I did cry.
BRUTUS	Yes, that thou didst. Didst thou see any thing?
LUCIUS	Nothing, my lord.
BRUTUS	Sleep again, Lucius. – Sirrah Claudio! [*To Varrus:*] Fellow,

Thou, awake!

VARRUS	My lord?	350
CLAUDIO	My lord?	
BRUTUS	Why did you so cry out, sirs, in your sleep?	
VARRUS, CLAUDIO	Did we, my lord?	
BRUTUS	Ay: saw you any thing?	
VARRUS	No, my lord, I saw nothing.	
CLAUDIO	Nor I, my lord.	
BRUTUS	Go and commend me to my brother Cassius;	

Bid him set on his powers betimes before,
And we will follow.

VARRUS, CLAUDIO   It shall be done, my lord.

[*Exeunt.*

ACT 5, SCENE 1.

The plains of Philippi.

Enter OCTAVIUS, ANTONY *and their* ARMY.

OCTAVIUS　Now, Antony, our hopes are answerèd:
　　　　　You said the enemy would not come down,
　　　　　But keep the hills and upper regions.
　　　　　It proves not so: their battles are at hand;
　　　　　They mean to warn us at Philippi here,
　　　　　Answering before we do demand of them.

ANTONY　Tut, I am in their bosoms, and I know
　　　　　Wherefore they do it. They could be content
　　　　　To visit other places, and come down
　　　　　With fearful bravery, thinking by this face　　　　　10
　　　　　To fasten in our thoughts that they have courage;[122]
　　　　　But 'tis not so.

Enter a MESSENGER.

MESSEN.　　　　　　　Prepare you, generals:
　　　　　The enemy comes on in gallant show;
　　　　　Their bloody sign of battle is hung out,[123]
　　　　　And something to be done immediately.

ANTONY　Octavius, lead your battle softly on,
　　　　　Upon the left hand of the even field.

OCTAVIUS　Upon the right hand I; keep thou the left.

ANTONY　Why do you cross me in this exigent?

OCTAVIUS　I do not cross you; but I *will* do so.[124]　　　　　20

*Drum sounds. Octavius, Antony and their army march. Drum sounds
beyond. Enter* BRUTUS, CASSIUS *and their* ARMY, *including* LUCILLIUS,
　TITINIUS *and* MESSALA. *Octavius, Antony and their army halt.*

BRUTUS　They stand, and would have parley.

CASSIUS　Stand fast, Titinius: we must out and talk.
　　　　　　　　　　　　[Brutus, Cassius and their army halt.

OCTAVIUS　Mark Antony, shall we give sign of battle?

ANTONY　No, Cæsar, we will answer on their charge.
　　　　　Make forth; the generals would have some words.

OCTAVIUS　Stir not until the signal.　　　　*[The four leaders meet.*

BRUTUS	Words before blows: is it so, countrymen?
OCTAVIUS	Not that we love words better, as you do.
BRUTUS	Good words are better than bad strokes, Octavius.
ANTONY	In your bad strokes, Brutus, you give good words: 30
	Witness the hole you made in Cæsar's heart,
	Crying 'Long live! Hail, Cæsar!'
CASSIUS	Antony,
	The posture of your blows are yet unknown;
	But for your words, they rob the Hybla bees,[125]
	And leave them honeyless.
ANTONY	Not stingless too?
BRUTUS	O yes, and soundless too;
	For you have stol'n their buzzing, Antony,
	And very wisely threat before you sting.
ANTONY	Villains, you did not so, when your vile daggers
	Hacked one another in the sides of Cæsar: 40
	You showed your teeth like apes, and fawned
	like hounds,
	And bowed like bondmen, kissing Cæsar's feet;
	Whilst damnèd Caska, like a cur, behind,
	Struck Cæsar on the neck. O you flatterers!
CASSIUS	'Flatterers'? Now, Brutus, thank yourself:
	This tongue had not offended so today,
	If Cassius might have ruled.
OCTAVIUS	Come, come, the cause. If arguing make us sweat,
	The proof of it will turn to redder drops.
	Look: [He draws.] I draw a sword against conspirators. 50
	When think you that the sword goes up again?
	Never, till Cæsar's three and thirty wounds
	Be well avenged, or till another Cæsar
	Have added slaughter to the swords of traitors.[126]
BRUTUS	Cæsar, thou canst not die by traitors' hands,
	Unless thou bring'st them with thee.
OCTAVIUS	So I hope;
	I was not born to die on Brutus' sword.
BRUTUS	O, if thou wert the noblest of thy strain,
	Young man, thou couldst not die more honourable.
CASSIUS	A peevish schoolboy, worthless of such honour,[127] 60
	Joined with a masker and a reveller!

| ANTONY | Old Cassius still. |

OCTAVIUS   Come, Antony; away!
– Defiance, traitors, hurl we in your teeth.
If you dare fight today, come to the field;
If not, when you have stomachs.
                    [*Exeunt, marching, Octavius, Antony and their army.*

CASSIUS   Why, now, blow wind, swell billow and swim bark!
The storm is up, and all is on the hazard.

BRUTUS   Ho, Lucillius! Hark, a word with you.

LUCILLIUS [*approaching:*]   My lord?
                                          [*They talk privately.*

CASSIUS   Messala!

MESSALA   [*approaching:*] What says my general?

CASSIUS   Messala,
This is my birthday, as this very day   70
Was Cassius born. Give me thy hand, Messala:
Be thou my witness that, against my will,
As Pompey was, am I compelled to set
Upon one battle all our liberties.
You know that I held Epicurus strong,
And his opinion;[128] now I change my mind,
And partly credit things that do presage.
Coming from Sardis, on our former ensign
Two mighty eagles fell, and there they perched,
Gorging and feeding from our soldiers' hands,   80
Who to Philippi here consorted us.
This morning are they fled away and gone,
And, in their steads, do ravens, crows and kites
Fly o'er our heads and downward look on us,
As we were sickly prey. Their shadows seem
A canopy most fatal, under which
Our army lies, ready to give up the ghost.[129]

MESSALA   Believe not so.

CASSIUS   I but believe it partly,
For I am fresh of spirit, and resolved
To meet all perils very constantly.   90

BRUTUS   Even so, Lucillius.   [*He turns to Cassius.*

CASSIUS   Now, most noble Brutus,
The gods today stand friendly, that we may,

Lovers in peace, lead on our days to age.
But, since the affairs of men rests still incertain,[130]
Let's reason with the worst that may befall.
If we do lose this battle, then is this
The very last time we shall speak together:
What are you then determinèd to do?

BRUTUS   Even by the rule of that philosophy[131]
By which I did blame Cato for the death   100
Which he did give himself (I know not how,
But I do find it cowardly and vile,
For fear of what might fall, so to prevent
The time of life):[132] arming myself with patience
To stay the providence of some high powers
That govern us below.

CASSIUS   Then, if we lose this battle,
You are contented to be led in triumph
Thoroúgh the streets of Rome?

BRUTUS   No, Cassius, no! Think not, thou noble Roman,
That ever Brutus will go bound to Rome: 110
He bears too great a mind. But this same day
Must end that work the Ides of March begun;
And whether we shall meet again, I know not.
Therefore our everlasting farewell take:
For ever, and for ever, farewell, Cassius!
If we do meet again, why, we shall smile;
If not, why then this parting was well made.

CASSIUS   For ever, and for ever, farewell, Brutus!
If we do meet again, we'll smile indeed;
If not, 'tis true this parting was well made.   120

BRUTUS   Why then, lead on. O, that a man might know
The end of this day's business ere it come!
But it sufficeth that the day will end,
And then the end is known. – Come, ho! Away!
                                                    [*Exeunt.*

SCENE 2.

Alarum. Enter BRUTUS *and* MESSALA.

BRUTUS   Ride, ride, Messala, ride, and give these bills
           Unto the legions on the other side.   [*Loud alarum.*
           Let them set on at once, for I perceive
           But cold demeanour in Octavio's wing,[133]
           And sudden push gives them the overthrow.
           Ride, ride, Messala: let them all come down.
                                              [*Exeunt separately.*

SCENE 3.

Alarums. Enter CASSIUS *(holding a standard) and* TITINIUS.

CASSIUS   O, look, Titinius, look, the villains fly!
           Myself have to mine own turned enemy:
           This ensign here of mine was turning back;
           I slew the coward, and did take it from him.
TITINIUS   O Cassius, Brutus gave the word too early,
           Who, having some advantage on Octavius,
           Took it too eagerly: his soldiers fell to spoil,
           Whilst we by Antony are all enclosed.

Enter PINDARUS.

PINDARUS   Fly further off, my lord; fly further off!
           Mark Antony is in your tents, my lord.   10
           Fly therefore, noble Cassius, fly far off.
CASSIUS   This hill is far enough. Look, look, Titinius;
           Are those my tents where I perceive the fire?
TITINIUS   They are, my lord.
CASSIUS   Titinius, if thou lovest me,
           Mount thou my horse, and hide thy spurs in him
           Till he have brought thee up to yonder troops
           And here again, that I may rest assured
           Whether yond troops are friend or enemy.
TITINIUS   I will be here again, even with a thought.   [*Exit.*
CASSIUS   Go, Pindarus, get higher on that hill.   20

My sight was ever thick: regard Titinius,
And tell me what thou not'st about the field.

[Pindarus climbs up.

This day I breathèd first; time is come round,
And where I did begin, there shall I end;
My life is run his compass. – Sirrah, what news?

PINDARUS   *[above:]* O my lord!

CASSIUS   What news?

PINDARUS   Titinius is enclosèd round about
With horsemen that make to him on the spur;
Yet he spurs on. Now they are almost on him.   30
Now Titinius. Now some light; O he lights too.
He's tane. *[A shout.]* And hark, they shout for joy.

CASSIUS   Come down; behold no more.   *[Pindarus descends.*
[Aside] O, coward that I am, to live so long,
To see my best friend tane before my face![134]
– Come hither, sirrah:
In Parthia did I take thee prisoner;
And then I swore thee, saving of thy life,
That whatsoever I did bid thee do,
Thou shouldst attempt it. Come now, keep thine oath.   40
Now be a freeman, and with this good sword
That ran through Cæsar's bowels, search this bosom.
Stand not to answer. Here, take thou the hilts,
And when my face is covered, as 'tis now,
Guide thou the sword. *[Pindarus stabs him.]* Cæsar,
                        thou art revenged,
Even with the sword that killed thee.   *[He dies.*

PINDARUS   So, I am free, yet would not so have been,
Durst I have done my will. O Cassius!
Far from this country Pindarus shall run,
Where never Roman shall take note of him.   50

[Exit.

Enter TITINIUS *(wearing a victory-wreath) and* MESSALA.

MESSALA   It is but change, Titinius; for Octavius
Is overthrown by noble Brutus' power,
As Cassius' legions are by Antony.

TITINIUS   These tidings will well comfort Cassius.

MESSALA　Where did you leave him?

TITINIUS　　　　　　　　　　　　All disconsolate,
With Pindarus his bondman, on this hill.

MESSALA　Is not that he that lies upon the ground?

TITINIUS　He lies not like the living. O my heart!

MESSALA　Is not that he?

TITINIUS　　　　　　　　No, this was he, Messala,
But Cassius is no more. O setting sun,　　　　　　　　　60
As in thy red rays thou dost sink to night,
So in his red blood Cassius' day is set.
The sun of Rome is set. Our day is gone;
Clouds, dews and dangers come; our deeds are done.
Mistrust of my success hath done this deed.

MESSALA　Mistrust of good success hath done this deed.
O hateful Error, Melancholy's child,[135]
Why dost thou show to the apt thoughts of men
The things that are not? O Error, soon conceived,
Thou never com'st unto a happy birth,　　　　　　　　70
But kill'st the mother that engendered thee.

TITINIUS　What, Pindarus! Where art thou, Pindarus?

MESSALA　Seek him, Titinius, whilst I go to meet
The noble Brutus, thrusting this report
Into his ears. I may say 'thrusting' it,
For piercing steel and darts envenomèd
Shall be as welcome to the ears of Brutus
As tidings of this sight.

TITINIUS　　　　　　　　Hie you, Messala,
And I will seek for Pindarus the while.　　[*Exit Messala.*
– Why didst thou send me forth, brave Cassius?　　80
Did I not meet thy friends, and did not they
Put on my brows this wreath of victory,
And bid me give it thee? Didst thou not hear
　　　　　　　　　　　　　　　their shouts?
Alas, thou hast miscónstrued everything.[136]
But, hold thee, take this garland on thy brow;
Thy Brutus bid me give it thee, and I
Will do his bidding. – Brutus, come apace,
And see how I regarded Caius Cassius.
By your leave, gods: this is a Roman's part:

Come, Cassius' sword, and find Titinius' heart.   90
                          [He kills himself.

Alarum. Enter MESSALA, BRUTUS, *young* CATO, STRATO,
        VOLUMNIUS, LUCILLIUS, LABIO *and* FLAVIUS.

BRUTUS   Where, where, Messala, doth his body lie?
MESSALA   Lo yonder, and Titinius mourning it.
BRUTUS   Titinius' face is upward.
CATO   He is slain.
BRUTUS   O Julius Cæsar, thou art mighty yet!
          Thy spirit walks abroad, and turns our swords
          In our own proper entrails. [*Distant alarums.*
CATO   Brave Titinius!
          Look whe'r he have not crowned dead Cassius.[137]
BRUTUS   Are yet two Romans living such as these?
          The last of all the Romans, fare thee well!
          It is impossible that ever Rome   100
          Should breed thy fellow. Friends, I owe mo tears[138]
          To this dead man than you shall see me pay.
          I shall find time, Cassius; I shall find time.
          Come therefore, and to Tharsus[139] send his body:
          His funerals shall not be in our camp,
          Lest it discomfort us. Lucillius, come,
          And come, young Cato: let us to the field.
          Labio and Flavius, set our battles on.
          'Tis three o'clock; and, Romans, yet ere night,
          We shall try fortune in a second fight.   110
                          [*Exeut with the bodies.*

SCENE 4.

Alarum. Enter BRUTUS, MESSALA, *young* CATO,
            LUCILLIUS *and* FLAVIUS.

BRUTUS   Yet, countrymen! O yet, hold up your heads!
                  [*Exeunt Brutus, Messala andFlavius.*
CATO   What bastard doth not? Who will go with me?
          I will proclaim my name about the field.
          I am the son of Marcus Cato, ho![140]

A foe to tyrants, and my country's friend.
I am the son of Marcus Cato, ho!

    Enter hostile SOLDIERS. *Fighting ensues.*

LUCILLIUS And I am Brutus, Marcus Brutus, I,
    Brutus, my country's friend; know me for Brutus![141]
                             [*Young Cato is slain.*
    – O young and noble Cato, art thou down?
    Why, now thou diest as bravely as Titinius,   10
    And mayst be honoured, being Cato's son.
                [*He fights two soldiers and is overcome.*

SOLDIER 1 Yield, or thou diest!
LUCILLIUS   Only I yield to die.
    There is so much that thou wilt kill me straight:[142]
    Kill Brutus, and be honoured in his death.
SOLDIER 1 We must not: a noble prisoner.
SOLDIER 2 Room, ho! Tell Antony, Brutus is tane.
SOLDIER 1 I'll tell the news. Here comes the general.

                Enter ANTONY.

    Brutus is tane, Brutus is tane, my lord.
ANTONY Where is he?
LUCILLIUS Safe, Antony; Brutus is safe enough.   20
    I dare assure thee that no enemy
    Shall ever take alive the noble Brutus:
    The gods defend him from so great a shame!
    When you do find him, or alive or dead,
    He will be found like Brutus, like himself.
ANTONY [*to soldier 1:*] This is not Brutus, friend, but, I assure you,
    A prize no less in worth. Keep this man safe;
    Give him all kindness. I had rather have
    Such men my friends than enemies.[143] [*To another
                        soldier:*] Go on,
    And see whe'r Brutus be alive or dead,   30
    And bring us word unto Octavius' tent
    How everything is chanced.
                            [*Exeunt.*

SCENE 5.

Enter BRUTUS, DARDANIUS, CLITUS, STRATO *and* VOLUMNIUS.

BRUTUS	Come, poor remains of friends, rest on this rock.
CLITUS	Statillius showed the torch-light, but, my lord,
	He came not back: he is or tane or slain.[144]
BRUTUS	Sit thee down, Clitus. Slaying is the word;
	It is a deed in fashion. Hark thee, Clitus. [*He whispers.*
CLITUS	What, I, my lord? No, not for all the world.
BRUTUS	Peace then, no words.
CLITUS	I'll rather kill myself.
BRUTUS	Hark thee, Dardanius. [*He whispers.*
DARDAN.	Shall I do such a deed?
	[*Dardanius and Clitus move aside.*

CLITUS	O Dardanius.	
DARDAN.	O Clitus.	10
CLITUS	What ill request did Brutus make to thee?	
DARDAN.	To kill him, Clitus. Look, he meditates.	
CLITUS	Now is that noble vessel full of grief,	
	That it runs over even at his eyes.	
BRUTUS	Come hither, good Volumnius: list a word.	
VOLUMN.	What says my lord?	
BRUTUS	Why, this, Volumnius:	
	The ghost of Cæsar hath appeared to me	
	Two several times by night: at Sardis once,	
	And this last night here in Philippi fields.	
	I know my hour is come.	
VOLUMN.	Not so, my lord.	20
BRUTUS	Nay, I am sure it is, Volumnius.	
	Thou seest the world, Volumnius, how it goes;	
	Our enemies have beat us to the pit.	
	[*Distant alarums.*[145]	
	It is more worthy to leap in ourselves	
	Than tarry till they push us. Good Volumnius,	
	Thou know'st that we two went to school together:	
	Even for that our love of old, I prithee,	
	Hold thou my sword-hilts, whilst I run on it.	

VOLUMN. That's not an office for a friend, my lord.

                                        [Nearer alarums.

CLITUS   Fly, fly, my lord! There is no tarrying here.   30
BRUTUS   Farewell to you; and you; and you, Volumnius.
        Strato, thou hast been all this while asleep;

                                    [Strato awakes.

        Farewell to thee too, Strato. Countrymen,
        My heart doth joy that yet in all my life
        I found no man but he was true to me.
        I shall have glory by this losing day,
        More than Octavius and Mark Antony
        By this vile conquest shall attain unto.
        So, fare you well at once; for Brutus' tongue
        Hath almost ended his life's history: 40
        Night hangs upon mine eyes; my bones would rest,
        That have but laboured to attain this hour.

                  [Loud alarums. The cry 'Fly, fly, fly!' *is heard.*

CLITUS   Fly, my lord, fly!
BRUTUS   Hence! I will follow.

                [Exeunt Clitus, Dardanius and Volumnius.

        I prithee, Strato, stay thou by thy lord.
        Thou art a fellow of a good respect;
        Thy life hath had some smatch of honour in it.
        Hold then my sword, and turn away thy face,
        While I do run upon it. Wilt thou, Strato?
STRATO   Give me your hand first. Fare you well, my lord.
BRUTUS   Farewell, good Strato.   *[Brutus runs on his sword.*
                  Cæsar, now be still;   50
        I killed not thee with half so good a will.[146]   *[He dies.*

Alarum. A retreat is sounded. Enter OCTAVIUS, ANTONY *and*
their ARMY, *with* MESSALA *and* LUCILLIUS *as prisoners.*

OCTAVIUS What man is that?
MESSALA   My master's man. Strato, where is thy master?
STRATO   Free from the bondage you are in, Messala.
        The conquerors can but make a fire of him;
        For Brutus only overcame himself,
        And no man else hath honour by his death.
LUCILLIUS So Brutus should be found. I thank thee, Brutus,

	That thou hast proved Lucillius' saying true.[147]	
OCTAVIUS	All that served Brutus, I will entertain them.	60
	[*To Strato:*] Fellow, wilt thou bestow thy time with me?	
STRATO	Ay, if Messala will prefer me to you.	
OCTAVIUS	Do so, good Messala.	
MESSALA	How died my master, Strato?	
STRATO	I held the sword, and he did run on it.	
MESSALA	Octavius, then take him to follow thee,	
	That did the latest service to my master.[148]	
ANTONY	[*of Brutus:*] This was the noblest Roman of them all.	
	All the conspirators, save only he,	
	Did that they did in envy of great Cæsar;	70
	He, only, in a general honest thought,	
	And common good to all, made one of them.[149]	
	His life was gentle, and the elements	
	So mixed in him that Nature might stand up	
	And say to all the world: 'This was a man!'	
OCTAVIUS	According to his virtue, let us use him	
	With all respect and rites of burial.	
	Within my tent his bones tonight shall lie,	
	Most like a soldier, ordered honourably.	
	So call the field to rest, and let's away,	80
	To part the glories of this happy day.	

[*Exeunt.*

FINIS.

NOTES ON *JULIUS CÆSAR*

In these notes, the abbreviations include the following:

c.	*circa* (Latin): approximately;
Cf., cf.:	*confer* (Latin): compare;
e.g.:	*exempli gratia* (Latin): for example;
F1:	the First Folio (1623);
F2:	the Second Folio (1632);
i.e.:	*id est* (Latin): that is;
O.E.D.:	*The Oxford English Dictionary* (2nd edition, 1989, and website);
Plutarch:	*The Lives of the Noble Grecians and Romanes*, translated by Sir Thomas North (London: T. Vautroullier and J. Wight, 1579);
S.D.:	stage-direction;
sic:	(Latin): thus: that's how it is given there.
S.P.:	speech-prefix.

In the case of a pun or an ambiguity, the meanings are distinguished as (a) and (b), or as (a), (b) and (c).

1 (Title) *JULIUS CÆSAR*: In F1, the full title is: 'THE TRAGEDIE OF IVLIVS CÆSAR.'

2 (1.1.10–11) *in respect . . . cobbler.*: 'compared with a fine workman, I am only what you would call a botcher'. The cobbler revels in puns: 'cobbler', meaning both 'botcher' and 'shoe-mender'; 'sole' and 'soul'; 'awl' (his tool) and 'all'; 'withal' and 'with awl'; 'recover' (restore, cure) and 're-cover' (patch).

3 (1.1.31) *triumph.*: triumphal procession in honour of Cæsar's defeat of Cneius and Sextus, sons of Pompey ('Pompey's

blood', line 51), at Munda in Spain in 45 B.C. Plutarch says that Cæsar's triumph offended Romans, 'because he had not over-come captains that were strangers, nor barbarous kings, but had destroyed the sons of the noblest man in Rome . . . '.

4 (1.1.37) *Knew . . . Pompey?*: Pompey the Great: Cneius Pompeius (106–48 B.C.), called Magnus ('the Great'). Once, with Julius Cæsar (his father-in-law) and Crassus, he had formed part of a ruling triumvirate; but, after Crassus' death, civil war took place between Pompey and Cæsar. Defeated at Pharsalus, Pompey fled to Egypt and was murdered there.

5 (1.1.65) *cer'monies.*: Though the F1 spelling is 'Ceremonies', in Shakespeare's works the word is usually trisyllabic, and *O.E.D.* admits 'sermonies' as one alternative spelling. My emendation eases the line's metre.

6 (1.1.67) *Feast of Lupercal.*: The Lupercalia was an annual Roman fertility-festival which probably originated in honour of Lupercus, an ancient deity sometimes identified with Faunus and Pan. During the festivities, two runners (naked except for goatskin girdles) wielded lashes, and any barren women thus struck were supposed to be rendered fertile.

7 (1.2.4) *Antonio!*: F1 sometimes uses this Italian form of 'Antonius', Mark Antony's Latin name. (F1 also names another character 'Claudio'.)

8 (1.2.19) *Ides of March.*: *Idus* (Anglicised as Ides) was the Roman term for the day deemed the mid-point of the month: the 15th day of March, May, July and October, but the 13th day of the other months.

9 (1.2.112–15) *Æneas . . . Cæsar;*: When the Greeks destroyed Troy after the legendary ten-year siege, Æneas carried his father, Anchises, on his back from the blazing city. Virgil's *Æneid* tells how, later, Æneas founded Roman civilisation. Cæsar was reputedly a strong swimmer, and Shakespeare seems to have invented this anecdote about his rescue by Cassius. (In line 115, 'tired' is pronounced disyllabically, '*tie*-erd', to pre-serve the line's metre.)

10 (1.2.119–21) *He . . . shake;*: Plutarch and Suetonius state that Cæsar's ailments included 'the falling sickness' (epilepsy): cf. line 251.

11 (1.2.136) *Colossus,*: The famed Colossus of Rhodes, a huge

bronze statue of the sun-god Helios, was erected *c.* 286 B.C. near the harbour, and was later believed (erroneously) to have straddled the harbour-mouth.

12 (1.2.152) *Great Flood,*: In classical legend, Zeus sent a deluge to destroy sinful humanity, but Deucalion and his wife, Pyrrha, were allowed to survive. Noah's Flood naturally comes to mind, too; and line 160 refers to the Devil of Christian tradition.

13 (1.2.155–6) *walks . . . room enough,*: Some editors emend F1's 'Walkes' as 'walls'. Line 156 offers a homophonous pun, for an Elizabethan pronunciation of 'Rome' was 'Room'. (In Shakespeare's *The Rape of Lucrece*, 'Rome' rhymes with 'doom' and 'groom'.)

14 (1.2.159–61) *There . . . king.*: 'Once there was a Brutus who would have tolerated the ruling presence of a king in Rome no more readily than he would have tolerated the rule of the everlasting Devil.' ('[K]eep his state' means 'hold court'; 'easily' means 'readily' or 'comfortably'.) Marcus Brutus claimed descent from Lucius Junius Brutus, foe of the royal house of Tarquin (Tarquinius), who took a leading rôle in the expulsion (in 509 B.C.) of Lucius Tarquinius Superbus, seventh and last of the kings of Rome, and his son Sextus, who had raped Lucretia. (See Shakespeare's *The Rape of Lucrece*.) The expulsion of the Tarquins established the Roman republic.

15 (1.2.186) *such . . . eyes*: 'such ferret-like (red and sharp) and such fiery-red eyes': an example of hendiadys (a rhetorical figure with a marked degree of duplication).

16 (1.2.185–8) *Cicero . . . senators.*: Marcus Tullius Cicero (106–43 B.C.) was a celebrated orator. Having supported Pompey, he was pardoned by Cæsar. After Cæsar's assassination, he openly supported the republicans, and was killed by soldiers of the triumvirate (Antony, Octavius and Lepidus). His death is mentioned in at 4.2.226–30.

17 (1.2.192–5) *Let . . . dangerous.*: Plutarch reports that though Cæsar felt untroubled by 'fat men and smooth-combed heads', he feared 'pale' and 'lean' men.

18 (1.2.213) *this . . . deaf,*: Cæsar's deafness was apparently Shakespeare's invention.

19 (1.2.220–22) *Why . . . a-shouting.*: Plutarch says that Antony

twice offered Cæsar a crown, and, though some spectators
applauded or cheered when it was offered, more applauded or
cheered when it was declined.

20 (1.2.261–2) *plucked me . . . cut.*:   The 'me' is an 'ethic dative':
it is logically superfluous but lends a colloquially personal
quality to the statement. The mention of the doublet is one of
several indications that Shakespeare's company wore Elizabethan (rather than authentic Roman) costume. Plutarch says
that Cæsar, 'plucking down the collar of his gown from his
neck, . . . showed it naked, bidding any man strike off his head
that would'. (On another occasion, he tore open 'his doublet
collar' and offered his throat for cutting.)

21 (1.2.282) *put to silence.*:   slain. (The dying Hamlet says: 'The rest
is silence.') Plutarch, however, says that Cæsar only deprived the
two of their tribuneships.

22 (1.2.311–14) *I will . . . Writings,*:   Plutarch says that these
writings were produced by Brutus' 'friends and countrymen'.
Shakespeare makes Cassius more Machiavellian.

23 (1.2.316) *Cæsar's . . . at.*:   The metre of this line may be
regularised either by making 'glanced' into 'glancèd' or by
sounding 'ambition' tetrasyllabically ('am-bísh-ee-òn'). Various
subsequent lines solicit the regularisation made by sounding as
two syllables the final syllable in a polysyllabic word (examples
being 'destruction' at 1.3.13, 'insurrection' at 2.1.69, 'impatience'
at 2.1.248, and 'satisfaction' at 2.2.73).

24 (1.3.15–18) *A common . . . unscorched.*:   This and some of the
other ominous events are described by Plutarch.

25 (1.3.26–8) *And yesterday . . . shrieking.*:   The bird is probably
the screech-owl, possibly the raven. The cry of each was
supposed to be a bad omen.

26 (1.3.126) *Pompey's Porch;*:   This *Porticus Pompeii* was a covered
area adjacent to the theatre which Pompey built in 55 B.C.

27 (1.3.128–9) *And . . . hand,*:   'and the disposition of the sky
gives it the same appearance as the task we are undertaking,'.
F1 has: 'And the Complexion of the Element / Is Fauors,like
the Worke we haue in hand,'.

28 (1.3.146) *old Brutus' statue;*:   the statue of Lucius Junius Brutus.

29 (1.3.152) *Pompey's Theatre.*:   *Theatrum Pompeii*, the first
permanent theatre in Rome.

30 (2.1.40) *Ides of March?*:   F1 has 'first of March?', probably a compositor's error.

31 (2.1.66–7) *The genius . . . man,*:   'the spirit and the bodily powers are then in debate, and a man's state,'. Editors often emend F1's 'of a man' to 'of man'.

32 (2.1.70) *brother Cassius*:   Cassius was Brutus' brother-in-law, for he had married Brutus' half-sister, Junia.

33 (2.1.73) *hats . . . ears,*:   Romans wore various kinds of head-gear.

34 (2.1.83) *If thou . . . on,*:   F1 has 'For if thou path thy natiue semblance on,': i.e., 'Because, if you follow your course, maintaining your natural appearance,'. Various editors emend 'path' (e.g. as 'hath', 'hadst', 'pass' and 'parle').

35 (2.1.166) *Let's . . . Caius.*:   Plutarch says that Brutus' intervention saved Antony's life, for all the other conspirators wished Antony dead, as he 'favoured tyranny', had great authority, and was popular with the soldiers.

36 (2.1.190) *There . . . him;*:   'There is nothing in him that we should fear;'.

37 (2.1.191) *Clock strikes.*:   The customary view that this is an anachronism is challenged by John Sutherland in *Henry V: War Criminal? and Other Shakespeare Puzzles*.

38 (2.1.204–6) *unicorns . . . toils,*:   Spenser's *Faerie Queene* (II.v.10) tells how a unicorn was caught when it embedded its horn in a tree. Bears could presumably be dazzled by means of mirrors ('glasses'). Pliny's *Historia Naturalis* (VIII.viii) says that elephants are caught by means of pits and trenches. The 'toils' are nets or snares.

39 (2.1.225–7) *Let . . . constancy;*:   Roman actors wore masks. The phrase 'formal constancy' means 'decorous reliability' or 'apparent consistency'.

40 (2.1.255) *I should . . . Brutus.*:   'I should not recognise you as Brutus.'

41 (2.1.261–2) *is it . . . humours*:   'is it healthy to walk about with your clothes unfastened and absorb the damp air'.

42 (2.1.283) *in sort or limitation,*:   'after a fashion or with restrictions,'.

43 (2.1.295) *Cato's daughter.*:   Marcus Porcius Cato, the Roman orator and statesman, was noted for his integrity. In the Civil

War, he joined Pompey; and, after the battle of Pharsalia, he continued to resist Cæsar in Africa. When Cæsar prevailed, Cato killed himself. Brutus was his both his son-in-law and his nephew.

44 (2.1.299–301) *I have made . . . thigh*::   According to Plutarch, Portia (troubled by Brutus' secret preoccupations) slashed herself in the thigh with a razor, in order to prove to her husband that she could bear and share pain. She sought to be his partner, rather than merely his 'bed-fellow and companion . . . , like a harlot'.

45 (2.1.S.D. after 309) *Enter . . . head.*:   In Elizabethan England, sick people sometimes wore kerchiefs on their heads. According to Plutarch, Brutus visited the ailing Ligarius, who said that he was fit to participate in any enterprise that Brutus might be planning. Plutarch calls him 'Caius' Ligarius, but his real name was Quintus Ligarius. He had fought for Pompey against Cæsar in the Civil War, but Cæsar had restored his rights.

46 (2.1.323–4) *Thou . . . spirit.*:   'You, like a magician, have summoned up my spirit, which previously was deadened.'

47 (2.2.17–24) *A lioness . . . streets.*:   Shakespeare derived these omens from various sources, including Plutarch and Ovid. In lines 19 and 23, F1 has 'fight' and 'do neigh', but numerous editors emend them as 'fought' and 'did neigh'.

48 (2.2.35) *It . . . fear,*:   The sense may be either (a): 'It seems to me most strange that men should fear it (the death mentioned just now)'; or (b): 'It seems to me most strange that that (death) should fear (i.e. frighten) men'.

49 (2.2.46) *We are . . . day,*:   F1 has not 'We are' but 'We heare': probably an error, though possibly an idiom meaning 'We are reputed'.

50 (2.2.76) *statua,*:   Here and at 3.2.187, though not at 2.2.85, 'statue' ('Statue' in F1) is trisyllabic, so, like some other editors, I change the spelling to 'statua' (Latin, and often English then, for 'statue').

51 (2.2.89) *For . . . cognisance.*:   'for coloured and stained objects, sacred relics and emblems.' (The noun 'cognisance' could mean 'symbolism', and here it may tacitly be plural: 'emblems'.)

52 (2.2.97) *Apt . . . say*:   'Apt to be rendered' means 'likely (or fit) to be made'. By preserving F1's 'some one' (an iambic foot)

instead of changing it to 'someone' (a trochaic foot), I keep the metre smooth.

53 (2.2.92–9) *I have . . . dreams'.*:   Plutarch says that the treacherous Decius told Cæsar that the Senate intended to proclaim him king of the Roman Empire outside Italy and to allow him to wear a diadem abroad; so, Decius asked, should the Senate really depart until Cæsar's wife 'should have better dreams'?

54 (2.2.S.D. after 107) *Enter . . . CINNA.*:   The S.D. follows F1. Some editors feel that Cassius should be present, so they substitute Cassius for Publius in the S.D. and in line 108. Publius is not one of the conspirators: see 3.1.89–95.

55 (2.2.128) *every . . . same,*:   This is proverbial in English ('All that is alike is not the same') and Latin. Here he means that to resemble a friend is not necessarily to be a friend.

56 (2.3.7) *security . . . conspiracy.*:   'over-confidence ushers in conspirators.'

57 (2.4.18) *bustling . . . fray,*:   'confused clamour like an affray,'.

58 (2.4.42) *O, . . . faint.*:   Plutarch says that Porcia (Portia) became so anxious that she swooned.

59 (3.1.8) *What . . . served.*:   Plutarch, however, says that Cæsar repeatedly attempted to read Artemidorus' warning, but so many people greeted him that he was unable to read it.

60 (3.1.13–24) *I wish . . . change.*:   This incident is described by Plutarch, who says that Brutus 'with a pleasant countenance' reassured the anxious Cassius.

61 (3.1.36–39) *These . . . children.*:   'This grovelling and deep bowing might suffice to make ordinary men become proudly impassioned, so that they treat capriciously, like children changing rules, what has been ordained and decreed since the earliest times.' F1 has 'the lane of Children'; most editors emend this as 'the law of children'.

62 (3.1.41–6) *thawed . . . way.*:   Walter Whiter's *A Specimen of a Commentary on Shakspeare* (London: Cadell, 1794), pp. 138–46, pointed out that Shakespeare often associates flattery and false followers with fawning dogs and melting sweets.

63 (3.1.47–8) *Cæsar . . . satisfied.*:   In his *Timber* (1612; rpt. London, 1641), p. 29, Ben Jonson deplored this assertion as he recalled it (possibly in an earlier version of the play): 'Cæsar

did never wrong, but with just cause'. (Jonson regarded it as
'ridiculous', though it is valid.)

64 (3.1.58–73) *I could . . . so.*:   Although Plutarch says that Cæsar
denied the conspirators' petition for Cimber, Plutarch offers no
counterpart to Cæsar's superb rhetoric here.

65 (3.1.74) *Olympus?*:   Olympus was, in legend, the Greek
mountain where the gods dwelt.

66 (3.1.S.D. after 76) Pompey's statue,:   Plutarch notes the irony
that 'it seemed that the image took just revenge of Pompey's
enemy'.

67 (3.1.77) Et tu, Brute?:   Literally, 'And thou, O Brutus?'; colloquially, 'Even you, Brutus?' or 'You too, Brutus?'. In F1, this is
'*Et Tu Brutè?*'. ('*Brute*' is disyllabic.) In his *De Vita Cæsarum*,
section lxxxii, Suetonius refers to reports that when Brutus
assailed Cæsar, the victim said (in Greek) 'You too, my child?',
Cæsar having enjoyed in the past a love-relationship with
Brutus' mother. Plutarch remarks that Cæsar had persuaded
himself that Brutus was his son. Like Cassius, Brutus had been
pardoned by Cæsar (who became his generous benefactor)
after being defeated in battle against him.

68 (3.1.105–10) *Stoop . . . liberty!'*:   Plutarch's description of
the killing and its immediate aftermath makes them sound
relatively confused and messy. As the conspirators crowded
round Cæsar, they accidentally cut each other: 'divers of the
conspirators did hurt themselves'; 'Brutus caught a blow on his
hand, . . . and all the rest also were every man of them
bloodied.'

69 (3.1.111–13) *How . . . unknown?*:   F1 has a question-mark after
'vnknowne' and, nearly three lines later, after 'dust'. In F1, the
question-mark sometimes has the function of an exclamation-
mark, so some editors prefer an exclamation-mark on both
these occasions. Either way, the passage is richly ironic. The
scene has often been re-enacted on stage; such assassinations
have often (usually execrably) been re-enacted in reality.

70 (3.1.136) *Thoroúgh . . . state*:   'through the risks of this un-
precedented state of affairs'. 'Thoroúgh' is disyllabic and, as
indicated, iambic ('Thor-*roo*').

71 (3.1.145–6) *my . . . purpose.*:   'my misgivings constantly prove
intelligently appropriate.'

72 (3.1.171) *(As . . . pity)*: 'Fire can be used to make a fire-barrier, and pity for the wronged people of Rome ("the general wrong") has overcome any pity for Cæsar.' (The first 'fire' is disyllabic, the second monosyllabic.)

73 (3.1.174–5) *Our . . . temper,*: 'our arms, which have been strong in enmity (against Cæsar), and our hearts, which are fraternal (towards you),'. Some editors have emended F1's 'strength of malice' to 'exempt from malice', 'in strength of amity' and 'unstrung of malice'.

74 (3.1.199) *Most noble,*: I take these words to be a sarcastic comment by Antony on himself. In F1, line 198 ends with a question-mark, which I have preserved. Some editors replace it with a comma, so that then 'Most noble' could apply ironically to the 'foes' of line 198 or reverently to Cæsar.

75 (3.1.204–6) *Here . . . Lethe.*: 'Here you were brought to bay, fine stag; here you fell, and here stand your hunters, marked by the ritual slaughter and made crimson by your bloodstream.' As often in Elizabethan literature, 'hart' puns on 'stag' and 'heart'. Deer-hunters were sometimes initiated by being smeared with the quarry's blood. (Plutarch says that Cæsar was 'hacked and mangled . . . as a wild beast taken of hunters'.) 'Lethe' (disyllabic, 'Lethee' in F1) is the name of the legendary river of Hades: the dead drink its waters and thereby forget the past. (Perhaps Antony implies that Cæsar's killers forget his achievements.)

76 (3.1.258) *hands*: F1 has 'hand'.

77 (3.1.271) *Ate*: Ate (disyllabic) was the Greek goddess of criminal folly and the avenger of sin; in Shakespeare she represents violent strife.

78 (3.1.273) *Cry . . . war,*: 'Havoc!' meant 'Let slaughter and pillage ensue!'. In *Henry V* (Prologue, 6–8), the 'hounds' of war are 'Famine, Sword, and Fire'.

79 (3.1.278) *Cæsar . . . Rome.*: Octavius Cæsar was the great-nephew, adopted son and principal heir of Julius Cæsar. He was eighteen years old at the time of the assassination.

80 (3.1.283) *catching, . . . eyes,*: F1 has 'catching from mine eyes,'. At 285, some editors emend F1's 'Began' as 'Begin'.

81 (3.2.12) *last.*: Brutus' ensuing speech is elaborately patterned, using numerous overlapping rhetorical figures. They include: parison (structural parallelism); antimetabole (phrases repeated

in inverse order); epanalepsis (the same word beginning and ending a statement); ploce (systematic repetition of a word within a statement); and anaphora (the same word beginning several clauses). Even a detail, the combination of the word 'Censure' with its inverted echo in 'your senses', resembles antimetabole.

82 (3.2.36) *shall . . . Brutus.*:   'than you may do to Brutus, should you require his death.'

83 (3.2.49) *Give . . . ancestors.*:   F1 allocates this line, and some subsequent lines in this scene, to Plebeian 2; but, as Plebeian 2 has departed to hear Cassius, editors usually re-number the plebeian speakers.

84 (3.2.75–7) *The evil . . . Cæsar.*   He refers to the proverbial notion that one evil deed lives on, exaggerated by report, while ten good deeds are forgotten. His 'So let it be with Cæsar' means, in context, 'May this be true of Cæsar (if you wish it to be)'.

85 (3.2.78) *ambitious*::   Throughout this speech, the word 'ambitious' is tetrasyllabic ('am-*bísh*-ee-ùs'), so as to maintain the pentameter.

86 (3.2.104) *brutish beasts,*:   'brutish' may pun on both the Latin *brutus*, meaning 'stupid', and the name 'Brutus'.

87 (3.2.172) *the Nervii.*:   Cæsar fought with conspicuous bravery when a Celto-Germanic tribe, the Nervii, was defeated by his forces in 57 B.C.; Antony was not present.

88 (3.2.182) *This . . . all;*::   The ungrammatical double superlative is for emphasis (as at 3.1.121). Plutarch says that Brutus stabbed at Cæsar's genitals ('about his privities'), making the cut particularly 'unkind' (unnatural), and more so if Brutus was indeed Cæsar's son.

89 (3.2.218) *wit,*:   F1 has 'writ', which F2 changes to 'wit'.

90 (3.2.223–7) *were I . . . mutiny.*:   Plutarch says that Brutus received 'quiet audience', though 'they were not all contented with the murder', whereas Antony's astute oration 'did greatly move their hearts and affections unto pity and compassion'. The people were told that Cæsar's will had bequeathed them 75 silver drachmas each and various gardens and arbours; then Antony eloquently praised the slain leader and displayed Cæsar's blood-stained clothing. The people, seizing benches and other wooden objects for the purpose, burnt Cæsar's body

in the market-place and used brands from the fire to ignite the assassins' homes. Plutarch says (twice) that the conspirators fled, but he also says that they 'locked themselves up safely in their houses'. Lines 226-7 distantly recall Luke 19:40 (Geneva Bible, 1560): 'I tel you, that if these shulde holde their peace, the stones wolde crye.'

91 (3.2.239) *seventy-five drachmas.*:   a substantial sum of silver coins.

92 (3.2.260) *He . . . house.*:   In reality, Octavius took about six week to reach Rome, and the triumvirate of Antony, Octavius and Lepidus was not formed until the autumn of the following year.

93 (3.3.1-2) *I dreamt . . . fantasy.*:   'Although I dreamt last night that I feasted with Cæsar, events give an ominous quality to that fantasy.' (In *Romeo and Juliet*, Romeo has a happy dream the night before his death.)

94 (3.3.33) *They . . . poet.*:   According to Plutarch, this poet (Caius Helvetius Cinna) was murdered by the mob. (Although 'turn him going' in line 32 means 'send him away', the previous and subsequent injunctions suggest lethal action, and F1's final S.D. for this scene, '*Exeunt all the Plebeians.*', leaves no hope for Cinna.)

95 (4.1.2-5) *Your brother . . . Antony.*:   Plutarch says that Antony, Octavius and Lepidus condemned to death two or three hundred (his figures vary) of the noblest men of Rome, and that Lepidus even acquiesced in the death of his elder brother. (In the event, Lucius Æmilius Paulus, this brother of Lepidus, although condemned, was able to escape.) Antony had no nephew called Publius, but his uncle, Lucius Cæsar, was among those condemned.

96 (4.1.9) *How . . . legacies.*:   Either (a) 'how to reduce the amounts due to be bequeathed (in order to increase our funds).', or (b) 'how to reduce our expenses by means of (our interpretation of) legacies.'

97 (4.1.14-15) *The three-fold . . . it?*:   The world, as known to Romans then, had three major parts, Europe, Asia, and Africa. The Roman Empire was divided by the triumvirate thus: Antony controlled Cisalpine and Transalpine Gaul; Lepidus, Old Gaul and Spain; and Octavius, North Africa, Sicily and

Sardinia. Plutarch remarks that the triumvirs 'did divide all the empire of Rome between them, as if it had been their own inheritance'.

98 (4.1.17) *our . . . proscription.*:   hendiadys again. A proscription was a decreed death-sentence; each victim had his property confiscated.

99 (4.1.20–22) *To ease . . . business,*:   Line 20 means: 'so that he will bear part of the burden of blame for our actions,'. In line 22, 'business' is trisyllabic ('busy-ness'), to maintain the metre. (In 4.2.298 it is disyllabic.)

100 (4.1.37) *objects . . . imitations*:   'sights, artifices, and second-hand items'. (Here 'imitations' has five syllables.) Some editors prefer 'abjects, orts' (i.e. 'rejects, scraps') to 'objects, arts'.

101 (4.1.40) *But . . . property.*:   'except as a tool.' Lepidus was eventually stripped of his powers by Octavius and put under close guard. *Antony and Cleopatra*, Act 3, scene 5, says that he has been seized and confined 'till death enlarge his confine'.

102 (4.1.44) *our means stretched;*:   'our means extended as much as possible;'. F1 has 'our meanes stretcht,'. Some editors emend this as 'our meinies stretched,' (i.e. 'our followers augmented,'), which improves the metre.

103 (4.1.48–9) *we are . . . enemies;*:   'we, set in our course and surrounded by many enemies, are like a bear in a bear-pit, tied to a stake and surrounded by barking hounds (or by hounds which hold us at bay);'.

104 (4.2.S.D.) *Drum . . . direction.*:   In this scene, F1 leaves ambiguous the deployment of characters, and editors vary greatly in their interpretations. The initial S.D. in F1 is: '*Drum. Enter Brutus, Lucillius, and the Army. Titinius and Pindarus meete them.*' Lucillius, however, seems to be with Pindarus and Titinius, for he tells Brutus about his reception by Cassius. Furthermore, Lucillius' initial command in F1, 'Giue the word ho, and Stand.', reciprocating Brutus' command to Brutus' soldiers (cf. lines 32–3), indicates that Lucillius, Pindarus and Titinius have an escort (perhaps of two or three soldiers). Some editors transfer Lucillius' order to a soldier who is an intermediary between Brutus and his army.

105 (4.2.7) *In . . . officers,*:   'either because his feelings have changed or because he has bad subordinates,'.

106 (4.2.S.D. after 52) *[Exeunt . . . tent.*:   Some editors begin a
      new scene at this point. In F1, however, the S.D. is: '*Exeunt /
      Manet Brutus and Cassius.*': in other words, while everyone
      else goes out, Brutus and Cassius remain on stage; so the
      action is continuous. Lucius and Titinius, ordered by Brutus
      to 'guard our door', may stand guard at the sides of the tent's
      entrance, which necessarily is very large (if the audience is to
      see clearly the interior).

107 (4.2.53–60) *That . . . comment.*:   Plutarch says that Brutus had
      condemned Lucius Pella for 'robbery, and pilfery in his
      office', and this annoyed the avaricious Cassius, who tolerated
      similar corruption by two of his friends. Cassius declared that
      Brutus should not be 'so straight and severe'.

108 (4.2.75) *But . . . robbers,*:   This seems to contradict what
      Brutus said at 2.1.19–21. According to Plutarch, Brutus told
      Cassius that Cæsar, though not directly corrupt, counte-
      nanced financial corruption.

109 (4.2.80) *bait not me;*:   i.e. 'do not harass me;': F1 has 'baite
      not me,'. Some editors emend this as 'bay not me.', i.e. 'do
      not howl at me.' or 'do not hold me at bay.'.

110 (4.2.134) *I denied you not.*:   Plutarch says that when Brutus
      needed money for his soldiers, he asked Cassius (whose funds
      were ample). Cassius' friends urged him to provide no
      money. Nevertheless, Cassius provided a third of the amount
      requested. (In financial matters, the historic Brutus was some-
      times ruthlessly extortionate.)

111 (4.2.153) *Pluto's mine,*:   Pluto (whose name means 'Wealth')
      was the god of the underworld, of gold- and silver-mines, and
      of corn. (Understandably, he was often confused with Plutus,
      god of wealth)

112 (4.2.160) *Do . . . humour.*:   'Whatever you choose to do,
      your dishonourable actions shall be deemed mere moodiness.'

113 (4.2.S.D. after 174) *Enter . . . him.*:   F1's S.D. is simply
      '*Enter a Poet.*', but the dialogue makes clear that he is strug-
      gling with Lucillius, and Lucius and Titinius (as guardians of
      the entrance) should play a part.

114 (4.2.183) *Ha . . . rhyme!*:   Plutarch says that the quarrel be-
      tween Brutus and Cassius was interrupted by the intrusion of
      the half-crazy Marcus Phaonius, who 'used [a] bold manner

of speech after the profession of the Cynic philosophers'.
(The Cynics, whose name derived from the Greek for 'dog',
scorned social conventions: see Apemantus in Shakespeare's
Timon of Athens.) Phaonius recited doggerel verse to the
leaders:

> My Lords, I pray you harken both to me,
> For I have seen moe years than suchie three.

Then 'Cassius fell a-laughing at him: but Brutus thrust him
out of the chamber, and called him dog, and counterfeit
Cynic'.

115 (4.2.185–7) *Bear . . . fools?*:   In line 185, 'fashion' is trisyllabic
to smooth the metre. Lines 186–7 mean: 'I'll tolerate his
eccentricity when he finds an appropriate time for it. Why
should warfare have any place for such foolish versifiers?'

116 (4.2.195–6) *Of your . . . evils.*:   'You make no use of your
philosophy, if you submit to misfortunes.' Brutus was a Stoic,
and Stoics strove to be unmoved by circumstances.

117 (4.2.197) *Portia is dead.*:   Brutus' response to Portia's death is
given in two forms, here, at lines 197–208, and subsequently,
at lines 231–245. (See the discussion on pp. 28–30.) Plutarch
says that when Portia was ill, she chose to die rather than
languish in pain; consequently, she put burning coals in her
mouth and kept it shut, so that she lethally choked herself.

118 (4.2.217) *Messala . . . letters*:   To improve the metre, some
editors accentuate the 'ed' of 'received'; but this is unnecessary,
as 'here' can be read disyllabically ('*he*-er').

119 (4.2.255–6) *Do stand . . . contribution.*:   The pentameter of
each line requires four syllables in 'affection' and five in
'contribution'.

120 (4.2.246–75) *What . . . Philippi.*:   Shakespeare derives
numerous details from Plutarch's account of the discussion in
which Brutus persuaded Cassius that they should fight
Antony and Octavius the next day instead of delaying.

121 (4.2.332) *Thy . . . L utus!*:   F1 has 'Thy euill Spirit *Brutus*?',
and, as was mentioned, F1's question-mark is sometimes
equivalent to an exclamation-mark. Some editors prefer a full
stop there. With variations, Plutarch says that 'a horrible
vision of a man' (not identified as Cæsar) appeared to Brutus

and declared: 'I am thy evil spirit, Brutus: and thou shalt see me by the city of Philippes.' This apparition, claims Plutarch, 'showed plainly, that the gods were offended with the murder of Cæsar'. Later, Brutus' men said that they had not heard or seen it.

122 (5.1.10–11) *With . . . courage;*: 'with a fine display which conceals fear [*or* with a terrifying display], thinking that by means of this show they will convince us that they have courage;'. Plutarch says that Brutus' army was notable for 'the bravery' (i.e. splendour) of its armour, much of it being silver and gilt.

123 (5.1.14) *Their . . . out,*: A Roman signal for battle was a displayed red flag. (In the play, 'battle' can also mean 'army' or 'battle-force', as in lines 4 and 16.)

124 (5.1.16–20) *Octavius . . . so.*: Shakespeare (to emphasise that both partnerships are discordant) has transferred a matter which, in Plutarch, involved Brutus and Cassius. There, Cassius granted Brutus' request to lead the right wing, even though people thought that Cassius, being older and more experienced, should lead it.

125 (5.1.34) *Hybla bees,*: The Sicilian region of Hybla was famed for its honey.

126 (5.1.53–4) *till . . . traitors.*: 'till traitors' swords have increased their total of slaughter by killing Octavius Cæsar too.' (F1 has the singular, 'Sword' of traitors.)

127 (5.1.60) *A peevish . . . honour,*: 'A silly schoolboy, unworthy of such an honour,'. Octavius was twenty-one at the time of the battle: Shakespeare compresses the time-scale of the sequence of historical events.

128 (5.1.75–6) *I held . . . opinion;*: Epicurus, a Greek philosopher who advocated personal tranquillity, claimed that the gods were indifferent to human activities and therefore sent no omens.

129 (5.1.78–87) *Coming . . . ghost.*: Plutarch says that two eagles, which had alighted on two of the foremost ensigns, flew away 'near to the city of Philippes'; and, later, men saw 'a marvellous number of fowls of prey, that feed upon dead carcases'. Such incidents 'began somewhat to alter Cassius' mind from Epicurus' opinions'.

130 (5.1.94) *affairs . . . incertain,*:   another instance of a singular
     verb linked to a plural subject.

131 (5.1.99) *that philosophy*:   Brutus' rule may derive from Plato,
     for, in his *Phaedo*, Plato reports the argument that the act of
     suicide is unlawful. (At line 111, however, Brutus says that
     he 'bears too great a mind' to submit to captivity, and he
     eventually commits suicide.) This passage follows Plutarch
     quite closely: for example, he reports that Brutus said: 'I
     trust (I know not how) a certain rule of philosophy, by the
     which I did greatly blame and reprove Cato for killing of
     himself . . . '.

132 (5.1.103–4) *prevent . . . life)*::   'anticipate the natural limit of
     life):'.

133 (5.2.1–4) *give . . . wing,*:   'give these written orders to our
     battalions on the far side of our army. Let them attack at once,
     for I notice that that side of Octavius' army shows little
     appetite for battle,'.

134 (5.3.28–35) *Titinius . . . face!*:   Plutarch tells how Brutus'
     forces succeeded, while Cassius' failed. Then Cassius, having
     bad eyesight, thought that Titinius ('Titinnius' in Plutarch)
     had been captured by enemies, when he had really been
     surrounded by joyful allies. Consequently, Cassius arranged
     for his bondman Pindarus to cut his head off; and 'after that
     time Pindarus was never seen more'.

135 (5.3.67) *Error . . . child,*:   because melancholy people imagine
     illusory woes.

136 (5.3.84) *Alas . . . everything.*:   Plutarch says that Titinnius
     arrived, crowned with a garland of victory, and, on discovering
     the misfortune which had befallen Cassius 'by mistaking', slew
     himself with his own sword.

137 (5.3.97) *Look . . . Cassius.*:   In this line, uncorrected copies
     of F1 say 'haue crown'd', corrected copies 'haue not
     crown'd'.

138 (5.3.99–101) *The last . . . tears*:   According to Plutarch,
     Brutus called Cassius 'the last of all the Romans', it 'being
     impossible that Rome should ever breed again so noble and
     valiant a man as he'. (Uncorrected copies of F1 have 'no
     teares' where corrected copies have 'mo teares'.)

139 (5.3.104) *Tharsus*:   F1 has '*Tharsus*', an alternative spelling of

Tarsus, an ancient city of Cilicia on the river Cydnus. Plutarch says that the body was sent to Thassos, an island off the coast of Thrace near Philippi.

140 (5.4.4) *son . . . ho!*: Cato's son was Brutus' brother-in-law.

141 (5.4.7–8) *And I . . . Brutus!*: F1 does not name the speaker of these two lines, but the later dialogue makes clear that the speaker is Lucillius, who (according to Plutarch, spelling the name 'Lucilius',) pretended to be Brutus in order to protect him.

142 (5.4.13) *There . . . straight*:: 'That I am so great a person will be a great inducement to you to kill me immediately:' or perhaps: 'Take this sum of money as a sufficient inducement to you to kill me immediately:'.

143 (5.4.28–9) *I had . . . enemies.*: Plutarch says that Antony remarked: 'I had rather have such men my friends, as this man here, than enemies.' (Subsequently, according to Plutarch, Lucilius served him faithfully.)

144 (5.5.2–3) *Statillius . . . slain.*: Plutarch says that Brutus thought that not many of his men were slain. To ascertain this, Statilius [*sic*] promised to go through the enemy's lines, and then, if all were well, he would show a torch-light before returning. Statilius did indeed show the torch, but was slain on the way back.

145 (5.5.23–S.D.) *Our . . . alarums.*: Brutus' 'beat us to the pit' means 'driven us to the edge of the grave.' (He alludes to the pit into which hunters would drive their quarry.) In the subsequent S.D., uncorrected copies of F1 have '*Loud Alarums*' where corrected copies have '*Low Alarums*'. There '*Low*' implies '*Distant*'.

146 (5.5.5–51) *Hark . . . will.*: Plutarch suggests that Brutus asked various comrades to assist his death, but they declined. These were Clitus, Dardanus, and Volumnius (who had studied with him). Eventually, according to one version, Strato held Brutus' sword 'and turned his head aside' while Brutus impaled himself on it. (In the other version, notes Plutarch, Brutus held a sword and fell on it.)

147 (5.5.59) *thou . . . true.*: At 5.4.21–2, Lucillius declared that Brutus would not be taken alive.

148 (5.5.66–7) *Octavius . . . master.*: Plutarch says that Messala

brought Strato to Octavius, and, weeping, said: 'Cæsar, behold, here is he that did the last service to my Brutus.'

149 (5.5.69–72) *All . . . them*.: According to Plutarch, Antony said 'that of all of them that had slain Cæsar, there was none but Brutus only that was moved to do it, as thinking the act commendable of itself: but that all the other conspirators did conspire his death for some private malice or envy . . . '.

GLOSSARY

Where a pun or an ambiguity occurs, the meanings are distinguished as (a) and (b), or (a), (b) and (c), etc. Otherwise, alternative meanings are distinguished as (i) and (ii), or as (i), (ii) and (iii), etc. Abbreviations include the following: adj., adjective; adv., adverb; conj., conjunction; e.g., for example; esp., especially; interj., interjection; intr., intransitive; *O.E.D.*, *Oxford English Dictionary*; pr., pronounced; tr., transitive; vb., verb.

abide: 3.1.94; 3.2.114: pay for.

abuse (noun): (i: 2.1.18:) misuse; (ii: 2.1.115:) corruption.

accoutred: dressed.

across: 2.1.240: crossed (a sign of melancholy).

action: 3.2.219: gesture.

addressed: 3.1.29: prepared.

advantage (vb.): benefit, profit.

afeard: afraid.

affections swayed: emotions ruled.

against: 1.3.20: near.

aim (noun): (i: 1.2.163:) guess; (ii: 1.3.52:) trajectory.

alarum: battle-noises.

alchemy: chemistry which strove to turn base metals into gold.

along: 3.1.115: at full length.

amaze: 3.1.96: bewilder, astound.

and (as conditional conj., e.g. at 1.2.263, 277, etc.): if.

angel: 3.2.180: (a) dearest friend; (b) attendant spirit.

annoy: molest, harm.

answer (vb.): (i: 3.2.80:) pay the penalty for; (ii: 4.1.47:) face; (iii: 5.1.1:) satisfy; (iv: 5.1.6:) challenge; **answer on**: respond to.

an't: 4.2.308: if it.

apparent: evident.

apply: interpret.

appoint: assign.

apt: (i: 2.2.97: a) likely; (b) fit; (ii: 3.1.160:) ready, willing; (iii: 5.3.68:) impressionable.

art: (i: 4.1.37:) artifice, cunning; (ii: 4.2.244:) theory.

astonish: dismay.

Ate (pr. *Ah*-tay or *Ai*-tee:) Greek goddess of misdeeds and vengeance.

awl: cobbler's piercing tool; **but with awl**: 1.1.22–3: (a) except with that tool; (b) but with all.

bade: (i: 1.2.106: a) invited; (b) told; (ii: 1.2.125:) told.

bang: **bear me a bang**: submit to being hit by me.

bark: **swim bark**: sail ship.

basis: pedestal of statue.

bastard: false Roman.

battle (noun): battalion, battle-force.

bay (vb.): (i: 3.1.204:) drive to bay; (ii: 4.1.49: a) bark at; (b) hold at bay; (iii: 4.2.79:) howl at.

bear (vb.): (i: 1.2.35:) maintain; (ii: 1.2.131:) carry off, win; **bear back**: move back;

bear hard: bear ill-will to; **bear it**: conduct oneself.

beholding: indebted.

bend (noun): 1.2.123: downward look.

bend (vb.): 1.2.117: bow.

bent (noun): direction.

betimes: early.

big: 3.1.282: swollen with grief.

bill: (i: 4.2.223:) decree; (ii: 5.2.1:) written order.

blaze (vb.): 2.2.31: (a) proclaim; (b) flame.

blood: (i: 1.1.51:) kin, stock; (ii: 1.2.151: a) stock;

(b) disposition; (iii: 4.2.166; 4.2.312:) disposition; **be let blood**: 3.1.152: (a) have blood surgically shed; (b) be slain.

blunt: (i: 1.2.291: a) dull-edged; (b) dull; (c) abrupt, harsh; (ii: 3.2.215: a) dull; (b) abrupt.

bondman: male slave.

bootless: fruitlessly.

bosoms: **am in their bosoms**: know their secrets.

brave (vb.): defy.

brave (adj.): 2.1.314, 322; 3.1.204; 5.3.80, 96: noble.

bravely: 5.4.10: nobly.

bravery: 5.1.10: (a) fine display; (b) defiance.

break with: 2.1.150: disclose to.

breed of noble bloods: heritage and stock of nobility.

brook (vb.): allow.

Brutus: **old Brutus**: Lucius Junius Brutus, foe of Tarquin.

calculate: forecast astrologically.

call in question: consider, examine.

cancel: annul.

Capitol: temple to Jupiter on the Capitoline Hill.

carrion (noun): carcase.

carrion (adj.): dead and rotting.

cast: 1.3.60: put.

Cato: Marcus Porcius Cato, Roman famed for integrity.

cause: 5.1.48: (a) matter in hand; (b) case to be argued.

cautelous: 2.1.129: (a) cautious; (b) crafty.

censure (vb.): 3.2.16: judge.

ceremony, cer'mony: (i: 1.1.65:) accessory of ritual; (ii: 1.2.11:) prescribed rite; (iii: 2.1.197; 2.2.13: a) ceremonial interpretation of omens; (b) omen.

chafing with: fretting against.

chair: 3.2.63: pulpit, rostrum.

change (noun): 5.3.51: exchange.

change (vb.): 3.1.24: turn pale.

charáctery: expression of thought by symbols (here, wrinkles).

charge (noun): (i: 4.1.9:) expense; (ii: 4.2.48:) troops.

charge (vb.): 3.3.2: load, burden.

charm (vb.): 2.1.271: (a) conjure; (b) entreat.

chase (noun): race.

check: 4.2.148: rebuke.

chidden: rebuked.

choler: anger.

chopped: chapped.

clean from: completely opposed to.

climate: region.

close (vb.): 3.1.202: agree.

closet: 3.2.129: (a) private room; (b) cabinet for papers.

cobbler: 1.1.11: (a) shoe-mender; (b) botcher.

cognisance: 2.2.89: (a) emblem or emblems; (b) symbolism.

cold: 3.1.213; 5.2.4: half-hearted.

colossus: gigantic statue.

colour: (i: 1.2.122: a) hue; (b) military 'colours'; (ii: 2.1.29:) excuse.

come by: 2.1.169: obtain.

commend me to: remember me kindly to.

commons: in commons: 4.1.27: (a) in public pasture; (b) among common people.

compact: agreement.

companion: 4.2.188: low fellow.

compass: circuit of time.

complexion: 1.3.128: disposition.

conceit (vb.): judge.

conception: idea.

condition: (i: 2.1.236:) bodily constitution; (ii: 2.1.254:) mental disposition; **make conditions**: 4.2.84: manage affairs.

conference: (i: 1.2.188:) debate; (ii: 4.2.17:) conversation.

confines: 3.1.272: region.

confound: 3.1.86: stun with dismay.

conjure: raise spirits by magical incantations.

conned by rote: memorised.

consort (vb.): accompany.

constancy: determination, resolution.

constant: steadfast.

constantly: steadfastly.

cónstrue: 2.1.307: explain.

consumed: destroyed.

contagion: 2.1.265: poisonous influence.

content: easy in mind, calm.

contrive: conspire.

contriver: plotter.

controversy: emulation.

corporal: corporeal, bodily.

corse: corpse.

costly: precious.

couchings: grovellings.

counsel: 2.1.298; 2.4.9: secret.

countenance: 1.3.159: (a)
approval; (b) noble face.

counter (noun): token or
debased coin.

course: race.

crave: require.

credit: 3.1.191: reputation.

crest: ridge of horse's neck.

cross (vb.): oppose.

cross (adj.): forked.

cull out: select.

cumber: harass.

curtsy: bow.

cut off: slain.

cynic: bluntly critical person.

damn (vb.): condemn.

danger: mischief, harm.

dart (noun): javelin.

dear (adj.): 3.1.196; 3.2.114:
keenly, to the heart; dearer:
more valuable.

deep (noun): depth.

degree: 2.1.26: (a) step, rung;
(b) rank, stage in ascent.

deliver: 3.1.181: declare to.

deny: 4.2.122, 129, 134, 155:
refuse.

difference: 1.2.40: (a) conflict;
(b) diversity.

dint: onset.

directly: 1.1.12; 3.3.9, 18, 19,
22: to the point.

discomfort (vb.): discourage.

discover: (i: 1.2.69): reveal;
(ii: 2.1.75:) identify.

disposed: 1.2.306: inclined to.

distract (adj.): insane.

doublet: tight jacket.

doubt: suspect.

drachma: silver coin.

drawn: 1.3.22: assembled.

drop (vb.): 4.2.125: shed.

dull: 1.3.57: obtuse.

durst I: if I dared.

earn: grieve.

elder: 2.2.47: stronger.

element: 1.3.128: sky;
elements: 5.5.73: constituent
parts.

emulation: envy, jealous rivalry.

enforce: (i: 3.2.38): exaggerate;
(ii: 4.2.163:) a) strike;
(b) provoke; enforced:
4.2.21: forced, strained.

enfranchisement: (i: 3.1.57:)
recall (from exile);
(ii: 3.1.81:) release from
servitude.

engage: pledge.

engagement: commitment.

enlarge: give vent to.

ensign: (i: 5.1.78:) standard;
(ii: 5.3.3:) standard-bearer.

entertain: take into service.

envious: malicious.

envy: malice, hatred.

Epicurus: Greek philosopher.

Erebus: a dark underworld
region.

eruption: unnatural calamity.

establish: appoint by decree.

eternal: inveterate.

even: (i: 2.1.133:) honest, straightforward; (ii: 5.1.17:) level.

excepted: 2.1.281: a specified exception.

exeunt: they go out.

exhalation: meteor.

exigent (noun): crisis.

exit: he or she goes out.

expedition: rapid march.

extenuated: understated.

extremities: acts of extreme violence.

face (noun): 5.1.10: bold front.

faction: adherents.

factious: **be factious**: gather followers.

fain: gladly.

fall: (i: 3.1.243:) befall; (ii: 4.2.26:) lower.

falling sickness: epilepsy.

false: 4.2.340: out of tune.

fantasy: (i: 2.1.197; 3.3.2:) imagination, fancy; (ii: 2.1.231:) phantasm.

fashion (vb.): (i: 2.1.30:) put a case; (ii: 2.1.220:) persuade.

favour: 1.2.91; 1.3.129; 2.1.76: appearance (esp. facial), aspect.

fearful: (i: 1.3.78:) frightening; (ii: 5.1.10: a) timorous; (b) terrifying.

fellow: (i: 2.4.20; 3.2.257; 5.5.45:) inferior person; (ii: 3.1.62; 5.3.101:) equal.

ferret . . . eyes: ferret-like eyes (red and sharp).

field: 5.5.80: army on the battlefield.

figure (noun): image.

fit: 1.2.120: shivering fit .

fixed and resting: immovable and changeless.

fleer: sneer.

Flood: Great Flood: Deucalion's Deluge.

flourish: fanfare of brass instruments.

force: **of force**: necessarily.

form: 1.2.295; 4.2.40: appearance, manner; **right form of war**: regular battle-formation.

formal constancy: 2.1.227: (a) decorous reliability; (b) apparent consistency.

former: 5.1.78: foremost.

Forum: public square and market-place.

fray: affray, fight.

fret: 2.1.104: interlace, pattern.

from: 1.3.35; 2.1.196: contrary to.

funerals: 5.3.105: funeral rites.

gamesome: 1.2.28: (a) fond of sport; (b) merry.

general (noun): 2.1.12: (a) republic; (b) public good.

general (adj.): 3.2.89; 5.5.71: public.

genius: tutelary spirit.

gentle: (i: 1.2.71; 5.5.73:) noble; (ii: 3.2.72; 4.2.319:) good, kind.

ghastly: pale, ghost-like.

give: given: 1.2.197: disposed;
  give place: 4.2.196: give in,
  yield; give way to: 2.3.7,
  4.2.91: give scope for.
glazed: stared, glared.
gone: 1.1.25: walked.
govern: control, direct.
grace (noun): 3.2.57: honour.
grace (vb.): do honour to.
gracious: virtuous, holy.
gravity: reputation for stability
  of character.
grief: 1.3.118; 3.2.210; 4.2.42,
  46: grievance.
grudge: ill-will.
hand: 1.2.312: hand-writing;
  at hand: at the start.
happy: 2.2.60: opportune.
hart: 3.1.204: (a) male deer;
  (b) heart, dear person.
hasty: fleeting.
'Havoc!': 'Let slaughter and
  pillage ensue!'.
hazard: on the hazard: at stake.
head: 4.1.42: resistance.
health: 4.2.88: safety.
heap: upon a heap: in a crowd.
hearse: coffin.
heavy: 2.1.275: sad, dejected.
hedge in: limit.
hie: hasten.
high: high east: due east;
  high-sighted: 2.1.118: (a)
  supercilious; (b) ambitious.
hilts: 5.3.43: three-part handle.
hinds: 1.3.106: (a) female deer;
  (b) servile people.
his: 1.2.124; 2.1.251; 4.2.60: its.
hold: 1.3.117: take this.

honest: honourable.
honesty: honour, integrity.
honey-heavy: laden with
  clogging sweetness.
honour: 3.2.15: integrity.
honourable (adj.): upright,
  honest; honourable (adv.):
  5.1.59: honourably.
hoot: 1.2.242: shout.
horrid: terrible.
hot at hand: eager at the outset.
how?: 2.1.312: how are you?
however: 1.2.295: although.
humour (noun): (i: 2.1.210;
  2.2.56; 4.2.98, 171:) mood,
  disposition; (ii: 2.1.250,
  4.2.160:) moodiness;
  (iii: 2.1.262:) damp air;
  (iv: 4.2.186:) eccentricity.
humour (vb.): 1.2.311: influence someone by flattery.
hurtled: clattered.
Hybla: Sicilian town famed
  for honey.
Ides: 13th or 15th day of the
  month; Ides of March:
  March 15th.
imitation: following fashion.
impatient of: unable to bear.
impossible: 2.1.325: apparently
  invulnerable.
improve: make good use of
  (O.E.D.).
incorporate to: united with.
indifferently: 1.2.87: (a)
  impartially; (b) calmly.
indirection: crooked means.
infused: imbued.
ingrafted: bonded.

instances: signs.
instrument: agent.
insuppressive: irrepressible.
intermit: delay.
issue: achievement.
itching palm: lust for money.
jades: 4.2.26: (a) worn-out
    horses; (b) vicious horses.
jealous: (i: 1.2.71:) suspicious;
    (ii: 1.2.162:) doubtful.
jigging: tritely-rhyming.
just: true.
keep: 1.2.307; 2.1.284: associ-
    ate.
kerchief: linen head-cloth.
kind (noun): (i: 1.3.64:)
    nature; (ii: 2.1.33:) species.
knave: lad.
knot: group, cabal.
knotty: gnarled.
know: 4.2.186: (a) acknowl-
    edge, (b) respect.
laughter: laughing-stock.
lay . . . off: take . . . off.
league: about three miles.
Lethe: underworld river of
    oblivion.
liable to: subject to.
lie: 3.1.286: lodge overnight.
lief: willingly.
light (vb.): (i: 1.1.55; 3.1.262:)
    fall; (ii: 5.3.31:) dismount.
like: 1.2.175, 251: likely.
limitation: a limited period.
list: listen to.
littered: born.
look about: be wary.
lottery: by lottery: arbitrarily.
lover: good friend.

low-crooked: bending low.
Lupercal: the Lupercalia, a
    fertility festival.
mace: official rod.
main (adj.): robust.
make: make head: raise an
    armed force; make our
    purpose: make our purpose
    seem; make to: make for,
    approach.
mark of favour: facial feature.
marry (interj.): by St. Mary.
mart (vb.): traffic in.
masker: participant in
    masques.
matters: women's matters:
    1.1.22: (a) women's con-
    cerns; (b) women's genitalia.
mean (noun): 3.1.161: means;
    by means whereof: in
    consequence of which.
mechanical (adj.): of the
    working class.
meet (adj.): fitting.
merely: entirely.
mettle: (i: 1.1.61; 1.2.292;
    1.2.305: a) temperament;
    (b) metal; (ii: 2.1.134; 4.2.24:)
    spirit, courage.
mischief: 4.1.51: hostile
    intention.
mistrust of: disbelief in.
mo, moe: more.
modestly: without exaggeration.
modesty: moderation.
monstrous: abnormal,
    unnatural.
mortal: 2.1.66: human.
mortifièd: deadened.

motion: 2.1.64: inward
prompting; **unshaked of
motion**: 3.1.70:
(a) unshaken by commotion;
(b) untroubled
by emotion.

mutiny: riot, revolt.

napkin: handkerchief.

native semblance: natural
appearance.

nature: **the nature of**: something like, a kind of.

naughty: worthless, vile.

neat's leather: animal-hide
(e.g. ox-hide).

new-added: reinforced.

nice: 4.2.60: trivial.

niggard (vb.): supply sparingly.

note (vb.): 4.2.54:
(a) stigmatise;
(b) publicly disgrace.

nothing (adv.): 1.2.162: not
at all.

notice (noun): information,
news.

object: 4.1.37: sight, spectacle.

observe: 4.2.97: offer homage
to.

occupation: 1.2.263: trade.

o'ersway: dissuade.

o'erwatched: wearied by
being kept awake.

offence: 2.1.268; 4.2.251:
hurt, harm.

offend: 3.2.30, 31, 33, 35:
injure.

Olympus: Greek mountain,
abode of the gods.

omit: miss, neglect.

once: 4.2.241: at some time.

only: 5.5.56: alone.

opinion: (i: 2.1.145:) reputation; (ii: 5.1.76:) view of life.

or . . . or: either . . . or.

orchard: 2.1.S.D.; 3.2.244:
(a) orchard; (b) garden.

order (noun): (i: 1.2.25;
3.1.230:) prescribed ceremony;
(ii: 4.2.230:) decree.

order (vb.): regulate; **ordered
honourably**: treated with
due honour.

ordinance: divinely-ordained
conduct.

out: (i: 1.1.16:) angry;
(ii: 1.1.17:) with worn-out
footwear.

palm: 1.2.131: emblem of
victory: palm-tree branch or
wreath.

palter: equivocate.

part (noun): function, duty.

part (vb.): (i: 2.1.193:) depart;
(ii: 3.2.4; 5.5.81:) divide.

passion: (i: 1.2.40, 48:)
emotion; (ii: 3.1.283:)
mourning.

path (vb.): proceed.

peevish: silly.

phantasma: nightmare.

Philippi: city of Macedonia.

physical: healthy.

piece out: fill, expand.

pit: 5.5.23: (a) hole to trap
animals; (b) grave.

pitch (noun): height.

pleasure: 3.2.246: pleasure-
ground, park.

pluck: pull.

Pluto: 'Wealth', underworld god, confused with Plutus, god of riches.

point upon: influence.

Pompey's Porch: portico of theatre built by Pompey.

portentous: ominous.

post (vb.): ride quickly.

posture: action.

power: 4.1.42; 4.2.219, 356: armed force.

prætor: magistrate.

prefer: (i: 3.1.28:) present; (ii: 5.5.62:) recommend.

preformed faculties: innate qualities.

present (adj.): 2.2.5: immediate.

presently: immediately.

press (noun): crowd.

prevail: have effect.

prevent: (i: 2.1.28, 160:) forestall; (ii: 3.1.35:) stop; (iii: 5.1.103:) anticipate.

prevention: forestalling.

prick (vb.): (i: 2.1.124:) incite; (ii: 3.1.216; 4.1.1, 3, 16:) tick, mark.

proceeding: advancement.

prodigious: ominous.

prodigy: remarkable and ominous event.

profess myself: profess my friendship.

profession: occupation.

proof: (i: 2.1.21:) experience; (ii: 5.1.49: a) clinching; (b) deciding by warfare.

proper: (i: 1.1.24:) fine; (ii: 1.2.41:) belonging; (iii: 5.3.96:) personal.

property: tool (*O.E.D.*).

proscription: death-sentence.

protest: proclaim.

provender: food for animals.

providence of: destiny allotted by.

puissant: powerful.

pulpit: (i: 3.1.80:) platform; (ii: 3.1.84, 229, 236, 3.2.S.D: a) pulpit; (b) chair on rostrum.

purpled: crimsoned (blood-stained).

purpose: **to the purpose**: to the point.

purpose (vb.): 2.2.27: determine.

put on: (i: 1.2.295:) assume; (ii: 1.3.60; 2.1.225:) disclose.

put up: 1.3.19: sheathed.

quality: character.

quarrel: legal accusation.

question: 2.1.13; 3.2.36: topic; **call in question**: examine.

quick: 1.2.29, 292: lively.

raise: 4.2.297: rouse.

range: rove in search of game.

rank (adj.): 3.1.152: (a) bloated; (b) corrupt.

rascal (adj.): wretched, poor.

reason with: 5.1.95: contemplate.

rebel (adj.): refractory.

recover: 1.1.24: (a) cure; (b) re-sole.

reek: steam.

regard (noun): esteem.
regard (vb.): (i: 5.3.21:)
  watch; (ii: 5.3.88:) honour.
remains (noun): remnants.
remorse: 2.1.19: (a) pity;
  (b) conscience.
repeal: recall from exile.
replication: echo.
resolve: **be resolved**: ascertain,
  be told.
respect (noun): (i: 1.2.59;
  3.2.15:) estimation, regard;
  (ii: 5.5.45:) reputation; **in
  respect of**: in comparison
  with.
respect (vb.): 4.2.121: heed.
resting: immovable.
retentive: confining.
retreat is sounded: trumpet-
  call halts a pursuit.
rheumy: dank.
right: 2.2.20: regular.
rive (vb.): split.
round: 2.1.24: rung.
rout: crowd.
royal: noble, munificent.
rude: uncivilised.
ruffle up: enrage.
ruled: 5.1.47: prevailed.
rumour: confused noise.
sad: 1.2.217; 272: serious, grave.
safe: 1.1.13: sound, clear.
satisfy: (i: 3.1.48, 141, 226;
  3.2.1:) justly convince;
  (ii: 4.2.10:).reassure.
saucy: insolent.
savage: wild, ungoverned.
scandal: slander.
scaped: escaped.

scarf: ceremonial band or
  ribbon.
schedule: document.
search: 5.3.42: pierce.
secret (adj.): discreet.
sennet: trumpet–call, fanfare.
senseless: insentient.
sensible of: capable of feeling.
sentence: **black sentence**:
  death sentence.
served: 3.1.8: attended to.
set: 5.1.73: stake, gamble; **set
  on**: (i: 1.2.11; 5.2.3:) proceed; (ii: 2.1.331; 4.2.356;
  5.3.108:) send forward.
several: (i: 1.2.313:) various;
  (ii: 2.1.138; 3.2.239; 5.5.18:)
  separate; **severally**: separately.
shadow: reflected image.
show (noun): (i: 1.2.34, 47,
  177:) appearance; (ii: 5.1.13:)
  display.
shrewd: malicious; **falls
  shrewdly**: strikes keenly.
silence: **put to silence**: killed.
sirrah (form of address): low
  person.
slight (adj.): petty.
slight off: treat with contempt.
slip: **let slip**: unleash.
smatch: flavour.
sober: calm.
soft (interj.): pause; **softly**:
  5.1.16: slowly.
soil (noun): blemish.
sooth: 2.4.20: truly.
sort: (i: 1.1.57:) class;
  (ii: 1.2.205:) manner; **in
  sort**: in a way.

sound (vb.): (i: 1.2.143:) utter; (ii: 2.1.141:) assess.

speed: 1.2.88; 2.4.40: give success to.

spleen: organ supposedly the source of passions; **venom of your spleen**: poison of your foul mood.

spoil (noun): (i: 3.1.149:) loot; (ii: 3.1.206:) skin of a slaughtered animal; **fell to spoil**: took to looting.

spot (noun): 4.1.6: dot.

spur: **on the spur**: at full speed.

spurn at: kick against.

stale (vb.): debase.

stand: (i: 2.1.142; 4.1.14; 4.2.255; 5.1.92:) be; (ii: 5.3.43:) delay; **stand up**: 2.1.167: make a stand; **stand on, upon**: concern oneself about.

stare: (i: 2.1.242; 4.2.92:) glare; (ii: 4.2.330:) stand on end.

start (noun): **get the start of**: take priority in.

start (vb.): 1.2.147: compel to emerge.

state: (i: 1.2.160:) regal splendour; (ii: 1.3.71; 3.1.136:) state of affairs; (iii: 2.1.67: a) state of affairs; (b) realm.

statua: statue.

stay (intr. vb.): 1.3.125, 136, 139; 2.4.2, 3; 3.2.149, 204: wait; **stay** (tr. vb.): (i: 2.2.75:) detain; (ii: 4.2.178:) prevent; (iii: 5.1.105:) await.

stem (vb.): plough.

still (adv.): constantly.

stir (noun): activity.

stomach: inclination.

strain: 5.1.58: lineage.

strange: 1.2.35: estranged, unfriendly; **strange-disposed**: extraordinary.

submit: expose.

success: result.

sudden: 3.1.19: swift.

sufferance: (i: 1.3.84:) patient endurance; (ii: 2.1.115:) suffering.

suit: petition.

suitor: petitioner.

sure (adv.): (i: 1.2.317:) securely; (ii: 4.1.47:) effectively.

sway (noun): realm.

sway (i: 2.1.20:) govern; (ii: 3.1.219:) divert.

swoonded: swooned.

tag-rag people: rabble.

take thought: 2.1.187: become melancholy.

tane: taken, captured.

taper: long candle.

tardy form: slow manner.

Tarquin: rapist expelled from Rome.

taste: **in some taste**: to some extent.

temper: temperament.

tempt: (i: 1.3.53: a) provoke; (b) test; (ii: 2.1.266:) risk; (iii: 4.2.88, 111, 114:) put to the test.

tending to: concerning.

Tharsus: city of Cilicia.

therefore: (i: 1.2.66: a) about that; (b) hence; (ii: 3.1.218:) for that purpose.

thew: sinew.

thick: 5.3.21: dim.

thing: 4.2.328: real entity.

thoroúgh: through.

thought: 2.1.187: melancholy; **with a thought**: 5.3.19: at once.

thunder-stone: thunderbolt.

Tiber: river flowing through Rome.

tide of times: course of ages.

time of life: natural limit of life.

tincture: colour-stain.

toil: net

token: sign.

touch (vb.): (i: 2.1.154:) harm; (ii: 3.1.7:) concern; (iii: 4.2.307:) play.

touching (adj.): grievous.

train: retinue, followers.

tributary: payer of tribute.

trick: 4.2.22: artifice.

trophy: honorific decoration.

true: (i: 1.2.257:) honest; (ii: 3.1.241:) correct.

try: 3.1.292: test.

turn: 1.2.56: reflect.

tut: not at all.

unbraced: unfastened.

undergo: undertake.

undone: not done.

unfirm: unstable.

unfold: disclose.

ungentle: discourteous; **ungently**: discourteously.

unkind: unnatural.

unluckily: 3.3.2: ominously.

unmeritable: undeserving.

unpurgèd: impure.

unsuppressive: irrepressible.

urge: (i: 2.1.155:) suggest; (ii: 2.1.243:) press; (iii: 4.2.87:) provoke.

use (noun): **beyond all use**: utterly extraordinary; **in use**: customary.

use (vb.): (i: 1.1.13:) practise; (ii: 1.2.72, 257:) be in the habit of; (iii: 5.5.76:) treat.

utter (vb.): emit.

uttermost: latest.

vaunt: boast.

venture (noun): 4.2.274: (a) merchandise risked at sea; (b) gamble.

vessel: (5.5.13: a) container, body; (b) human being.

vilde, vile: (i: 1.3.111:) worthless; (ii: 2.1.265:) foul; (iii: 3.2.32; 4.2.123; 5.1.39, 102; 5.5.38:) base, low.

vildely: vilely.

virtue: 1.2.90; 2.1.133, 269; 5.5.76: merit.

voice: 3.1.177; 4.1.16: (a) vote; (b) opinion.

void: **more void**: relatively empty.

vulgar (noun): common people.

wafter: wafture: waving.

warn: 5.1.5: challenge.

watch (vb.): 4.2.299: stay awake to serve.

watchful: causing insomnia.

weigh: 2.1.108: consider.

well given: well disposed.

when?: 2.1.5: hurry!

whe'r: whether.

where: 1.2.59: that.

while: **woe the while**: alas for these times; **whiles**: 1.2.209: while.

will (noun): 3.3.3; 4.2.274; 5.3.48: desire, wish.

wind (vb.): turn.

window: 3.2.255: shutter.

wit: (i: 1.2.296:) intelligence; (ii: 3.2.218: a) invention; (b) cleverness.

withal: 2.1.249, 292, 294: in addition, besides.

woe the while: alas for these times.

word: 4.2.2, 33; 5.3.5: word of command.

work (vb.): (i: tr.: 1.2.163:) move, influence; (ii: intr.: 2.1.209; 3.2.256:) proceed.

worthy: important; **worthy note**: noteworthy.

wrong: 3.1.242: harm.

yoke and sufferance: servitude and patience.